USING
ENGLISH
TO LEARN
MANDARIN CHINESE

The JWK Method
(Software Patent-Pending)

Jenwei Kuo

Using English to Learn Mandarin Chinese

Jenwei Kuo is a native Chinese and has lived in the United States for almost thirty years. During this time, he dedicated himself to the search for a solution that would eliminate language acquisition barriers and facilitate the learning and teaching of Chinese. Although the JWK method has come to fruition in this book, Mr. Kuo's endeavor still continues. Teaching Chinese to English-speaking adults is both his passion and hobby. Currently, Mr. Kuo is the principal of a Chinese language school.

ISBN: 978-0-6152-1044-5

Acknowledgments

I wish to thank my wife Kouchen for her continuous encouragement and support. I would like to thank Dr. James R. Philips, Mr. Luke Chen, Ms. Jennifer Libby, and Mr. James Kuo for their review and editing work, and my students at IBM at RTP/NC and North Carolina Raleigh Chinese Language School for their candid critiques. I also wish to thank Mr. James Kuo for his art design of the book covers.

Contents

Appendix C: Amusing Skits for Conversation Fun & Practice

Index

1

About This Book

Mandarin is the most common language spoken among Chinese people. The official name for Mandarin in China is 'Pu Tong Hua,' whereas in Taiwan it is called 'Guo Yu.' In this book, we will use the more collective term – Chinese – to mean all the above.

You probably believe that Chinese is hard to learn. However, you will see learning Chinese in a different light after completing the following exercise. Please use an English to Chinese dictionary to find and verify the Chinese words for the following sentences:

1	I	drink	tea.
2	Wǒ	hē	chá.

3	I	drink	tea.	I	also	drink	coffee.
4	Wǒ	hē	chá.	Wǒ	yě	hē	kāfēi.

5	I	do	not	drink	tea,	but	I	drink	coffee.
6	Wǒ	—	bù	hē	chá,	dànshì	wǒ	hē	kāfēi.

7	I	am	a	football	fan.
8	Wǒ	shì (be)	yíge	zúqiú	mí.

9	My	teacher	teaches	me	how	to	fish.
10	Wǒde	lǎoshī	jiāo	wǒ	rúhé	—	diàoyú.

11	Do	you	fish	?
12	--	Nǐ	diàoyú	ma?

In the exercise, you may find that the Chinese language rules are much simpler, such as that the auxiliary verb 'do' does not have its counterpart in Chinese; that no distinction is in Chinese for the verb 'to be' group of words: is, am, are, was, and were; that no different words are for subjective (I) and objective (me) pronouns. In addition, have you noticed any one-to-one correlation between English and Chinese?

This correlation is found even in longer sentences:

13	Last	night	I	had	a	nightmare.	I	dreamed	that	I
14	Zuó	wǎn	wǒ	zuò le	yíge	èmèng.	wǒ	mèngjiàn le	—	wǒ

15	fell	into	a	black	hole,	and	no	one	came	to	rescue	me.
16	diào	jìn le	yíge	hēi	dòng,	—	méiyǒu	yíge	lái	—	jiù	wǒ.

If you check, you will find that in Chinese the present (have) and past (had) tenses share the same word 'have;' there is no infinitive (no need to cope with the word 'to' before the word 'rescue'). Consequently, you see that a significant correlation exists between the English and Chinese language structures, as just demonstrated. Interestingly, even the number of syllables are mostly equal and sometimes one more or one less.

In fact, many languages that come from a common root language have a high degree of natural correlation. For example, French, Spanish, Italian, and Portuguese share a Latin language foundation. In general, languages sharing a common root language may consistently experience a high degree of language structure correlation and thus may be much easier to learn. However, it is quite a surprise that an Eastern language like Chinese, lacking a common root language with the Western language English, still has a high degree of grammatical correlation with English. A new method (the JWK method, software patent-pending) arises from recognizing this characteristic and provides a holistic view and a systematic approach to facilitate Chinese language learning and teaching. Interestingly, the spirit of this method can be equally applicable to 'using Chinese to learn English.'

1.1 The JWK Method – Using English To Learn Chinese

This method begins by using English patterns that you are familiar with as the *foundation* and overlaying the Chinese counterparts. It is amazing to discover the similarities between Chinese and English language structures. For the most part, the two have either the same patterns (one-to-one mapped) or are systematically backwards to each other (reversely mapped). Although cultural-specific elements are inevitable, the general relationship still holds and does not move beyond our ability to learn Chinese via English. In technical terms, this method places the two languages side-by-side to systematically compare and identify the direct correlation, cross correlation, and culture-specific factors. As a result, this new method contributes significant savings in time and money.

How does the JWK method differ from conventional Chinese learning methods? This method teaches students how to speak Chinese by using the same knowledge base an English-speaking student already uses to speak his or her native language. As a result, students can quickly learn to communicate in Chinese as easily as they do in English. Conventional methods focus on 'point-application' subjects, such as 'Greetings,' 'Introduction,' 'At School,' 'In A Restaurant,' etc., in which the scope is limited, and students may not be able to expand the 'canned' lines to other applications.

This book is designed as a must-read tool book for English-speaking students who are about to embark on their Chinese language learning journey and want to learn Chinese in a short period of time. The JWK method first helps to eliminate the fear of learning Chinese, a language often considered to be difficult to learn. Next, it prepares students to establish a learner-friendly mindset by helping them to recognize Chinese as a familiar language. Finally, using English as a foundation, the method naturally eases students into learning and mastering the Chinese language in a considerably shorter time frame.

Will this book replace books on conventional methods? This book and the conventional method books are complementary. This book is the *first step tool* that equips students with a solid Chinese language framework, an element so critical that it enables unprecedented time and money savings. After completing this book, students may continue on with 'point-application' based conventional method books where more application-specific vocabulary may be obtained, if not covered in this book.

The purpose of this book is to teach learners how to understand and speak Chinese. We encourage students to boldly mix English and Chinese words initially when speaking. Doing so helps students practice Chinese structure and vocabulary at an early stage and grow into speaking full-Chinese sentences as learning continues.

We are excited to see this proven method revolutionizes how Chinese is taught and learned!

1.2 How to use this book

In addition to this book, an English-Chinese dictionary and a few pronunciation web sites will be sufficient to help you become fluent in Chinese within a short period of time, depending upon the aggressiveness of your vocabulary building plan.

Examining the diagram below, we see that the majority of Chinese sentences can be constructed via your English knowledge and through the use of an English-Chinese dictionary and the direct correlation and cross correlation mappings elaborated in this book.

This book includes four parts: (1) Direct Correlation, (2) Cross Correlation, (3) Culture-specific elements, and (4) Pronunciation.

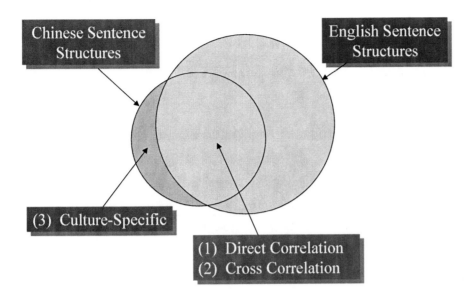

The Chinese **pronunciation** system – Pinyin – is covered in Chapter 2, and endeavors to match each Chinese sound element (vowel, consonant, tone) with an English equivalent to facilitate learning. There are also several web sites provided at the end of this chapter to assist you in pronunciation practices.

The **Direct Correlation** part is elaborated in Chapter 3 in various self-explanatory tables to provide a systematic comparison between English and its Chinese counterparts. For example, the following tables demonstrate that you can construct any sentence in 'subject + verb(s) + object' structures, which are fully correlated between English and Chinese. In addition, Chinese does not have singular, plural, verb/subject agreement, verb conjugation, and many other rules as English does.

	subject	verb	object
English:	I	drink	coffee.
Chinese:	Wǒ	hē	kāfēi.
English:	We	play	basketball.
Chinese:	Wǒmen	dǎ	lánqiú.

	subject	verb $_1$	verb $_2$		verb $_3$	object	
English:	You	may	come	to	pickup	your	tickets.
Chinese:	Nǐ	néng	lái	–	ná	nǐde	piào.

The following table illustrates a simple example for a cross correlation. The adjective phrase in English is often positioned <u>after</u> the noun it modifies. However, the adjective phrase in Chinese comes <u>before</u> the noun it modifies. Thus a cross correlation relationship is formed, but the rest of the sentence remains directly correlated as shown. Note that 'de' (的) is an additive for an adjective phrase, and that no article 'the' exists in Chinese. The **Cross Correlation** part is detailed in Chapter 4.

	noun		adjective phrase			
English:	The book		*on the table*		is	mine.
	adjective phrase		**noun**			
Chinese:	*Zài zhuōzi shàng*	de	shū		shì	wǒde.

Culture-specific elements are embedded throughout the chapters as 'culture-specific notes' and also illustrated in Chapter 8. As shown in the table below, 'bǎ' is a culture-specific element for which no English counterpart exists. Line (1) is directly correlated with its English counterpart and already is very good Chinese, i.e. no wording or structural errors; however, Chinese people would probably use line (2) by introducing a *culture-specific element* 'bǎ' along with relocating the verb to sit after the object.

bǎ						
	subject		**verb**	**object**		
English:	He		mopped	the	floor.	
(1) Very good Chinese:	Tā		cā le	–	dìbǎn	
		additive				**verb**
(2) Chinese Chinese:	Tā	bǎ	–	–	dìbǎn	cā le.

This book also includes numerous exercises placed immediately after each pattern structure. We recommend that students complete these exercises to reinforce the illustrated key points.

Exercise						
	subject		**verb**	**object**		
English:	That dog		ate	my ice cream!		
(1) Very good Chinese:	Nàzhī gǒu		chī le	wǒde bīng qílín!		
		additive				**verb**
(2) Chinese Chinese:	Nàzhī gǒu	bǎ	–	wǒde bīng qílín	chī le!	

You may ask, "Can English culture-specific elements, i.e. the English idioms, be used as the foundation for the correlation?" The answer is that you must avoid using English idiomatic expressions but use English baseline equivalents instead.

In summary, a key strategy of this book is to use the already-familiar English language structure as a *foundation* on which we build the learning of Chinese via applying direct correlation, cross correlation, and culture-specific components. We use self-explanatory tables for side-by-side comparison. In this way, we are able to teach the Chinese language structure without introducing 'Chinese Grammar' terms; thus removing a time-consuming heavy and complex burden. Only basic

English grammar terms are used. Consequently, students are able to spend more time on pronunciation practice and vocabulary building, speeding progress and thereby encouraging success.

The four parts of this book are broken down into following chapters:

Chapter 1:   About this book

Chapter 2:   Pinyin – The Chinese Pronunciation System

Chapter 3:   Direct Correlations between English and Chinese

Chapter 4:   Cross Correlations between English and Chinese

Chapter 5:   How English Questions Correlate with their Chinese Counterpart

Chapter 6:   How English Tenses Correlate with their Chinese Counterpart

Chapter 7:   How English Conjunctions Correlate with their Chinese Counterpart

Chapter 8:   Culture-Specific Chinese Words & Phrases

Appendix A: A Quick Reference for Handy Conversation Lines

Appendix B: Vocabulary Building Blocks

Appendix C: Amusing Skits for Fun and Practice

1.3   Conventions

Optional [...]:   It means that the content 'hěn (very)' in the bracket [hěn (very)] is optional.

Or /:   It means that the subjects in the sentence, 'I (Wǒ)/You (Nǐ)/She/He (Tā) drink tea.' can be 'I (Wǒ) or You (Nǐ) or She (Tā) or He (Tā).'

2

Hànyǔ Pīnyīn – The Chinese Pronunciation System

Hànyǔ Pīnyīn, or just Pīnyīn, is the most popular Roman alphabet-based Chinese pronunciation system. For example, Chinese characters (words) '中' and '文' are represented in Pīnyīn as 'zhōng' and 'wén' respectively. Although Pīnyīn's Roman alphabet words may look very much like English, the pronunciation is significantly different. This chapter introduces Pīnyīn so that you will be able to pronounce 'zhōng' and 'wén' correctly.

The Chinese pronunciation system includes three basic elements: (1) **vowels**, (2) **consonants**, and (3) the **five tones**.

As in English, Chinese also makes use of consonant and vowel combination for pronunciation. Although different names are used in the Pīnyīn system to describe consonants (initials) and vowels (finals), we will continue to use the English terms in this book to maintain familiarity.

In Pīnyīn, as in English, a syllable is a sound pronounced via a vowel, or a consonant followed by a vowel. In Chinese, a syllable is used to pronounce a Chinese character (e.g. 我 = wǒ = I). The purpose of this book is to use Pīnyīn as the medium to teach learners to understand and speak Chinese. Therefore, instead of using the Chinese character '我,' we represent the English word 'I' in Pīnyīn syllable form 'wǒ.' In order to provide learners with a good association between the English and Chinese counterparts, multiple Chinese syllables may be grouped together to match with a single English word. For example, the English word 'today' maps to two individual Chinese characters, that are, in Pīnyīn syllables, 'jīn' (今) and 'tiān' (天), but are represented as 'jīntiān.'

Another key aspect of Chinese pronunciation is the tones, such as the small marks: ¯ and ´, appearing on top of 'o' and 'e' in 'zhōng' (中) and 'wén' (文) respectively. Tone accuracy is the dominant factor that controls a speaker's accent and fluency.

This book endeavors to make learning these three elements of pronunciation easy and fun by giving each sound an English equivalent or close approximation.

In addition, one tip to accurate Chinese pronunciation is to speak 'one syllable at a time,' which means that the first syllable sound does *not* bleed into the second syllable, or vice versa. For example, in 'Pick it up,' it is legitimate to pronounce 'Pic ki tup' in English, but no bleeding is allowed in Chinese. Another tip is that English pronunciation may have a 'tail' following a syllable, but 'no tail' is there for Chinese. By referring to the following tables and exercising these and other tips to be provided, you will soon enjoy the victory of being able to speak Chinese well.

2.1   The Five Tones

Chinese is a tonal language, which means that a single syllable sound can be pronounced in various tones and each carries a different meaning. There are five tones. English has tones as well, so we use an English equivalent for each tone as summarized in the following. The provided 'English Equivalents' have been proven to be helpful to learners trying to master the five tones.

n^{th} Tone	English Equivalent	Tone Mark	Description
1	Ahh…….	—	A steady and extended tone, going neither up or down.
2	Huhh…?	/	A rising tone like when you are confused.
3	Uh-huhh…	✓	A downward then upward tone.
4	Hey!	\	A downward tone.
Neutral	A staccato note	(blank)	A short and light tone.

A self-explanatory tone graph is shown below.

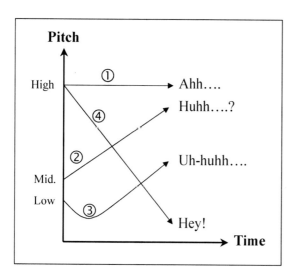

Uttering a tone is similar to singing a musical note. Depending on the note in the music, you start with a pitch and then extend it upward, downward, or hold steady as the time goes. In the same way, each of the four tones has its own starting pitch as shown in the diagram, where the highest starting pitch varies depending on speaker's comfortable vocal range. The 1st tone has the highest starting pitch and holds the pitch steady with time. It is like when your doctor asks you to open wide and say, "Ahh....", and you utter it in a steady pitch and extend the sound for a period of time. The 2nd tone starts at middle pitch and traverses upward as you say, "Huhh....?" The 3rd tone starts at the lowest starting pitch. It goes downward and then swings back up, like when you say, "Uh-huhh...." Imaging that you are listening to your daughter and acknowledging her as she is telling you a funny story that happened in school. The 4th tone has the same starting pitch as the 1st tone and traverses downward like when you exclaim, "Hey!"

2.2   Vowels

A summary of all the vowels in Pīnyīn is presented in the following table. You may scan it or study it now, but should refer back to it as often as necessary until you can automatically reproduce the correct sounds. In Pīnyīn, there are single-letter vowels, such as: a, e, i, o, u and ü, and multi-letter vowels, such as: ao, ia, ie, iao, ou, eng, iang, iong, uang, etc. Do not become overwhelmed by the number of vowels. As shown in the fourth column in the table below, 'English Equivalents' are provided to help you pronounce Pīnyīn effortlessly. The third column indicates the Pīnyīn representation when the vowel *stands alone* as a syllable, where a '—' indicates that there is no such vowel standalone as a syllable.

Pīnyīn		English Equivalent	Vocabulary Examples
Basic Unit	Stand Alone		
a	a	<u>fa</u>ther	à (ah), dà (big), jiā (home)
ai	ai	<u>I</u>	ài (love), hái (also, in addition)
an	an	w<u>an</u>d	ān (peace), wǔ ān (good afternoon)
ang	ang	<u>youn</u>g	áng guì (expensive), Shànghǎi
ao	ao	c<u>ow</u>	áo (boil), yào (want), xūyào (need)

V o w e l s	e	e	c<u>u</u>p	**è** (hungry), ch**ē** (vehicle), h**ē** (drink)
	ei	ei	l<u>ay</u>	**èi** (hey), l**èi** (tired)
	en	en	Sound of <u>n</u>	**ēn** (mercy), M**ě**iguó r**én** (American)
	eng	—	l<u>ung</u>	l**ě**ng (cold), n**é**ng (can), f**ē**ng (wind)
	er	er	t<u>er</u>se	**èr** (two), yīdiǎn**r** (a little bit, silent n)
	i	**yi**	<u>ee</u>l	**yī** (one), j**ī** (chicken)
	ia	**ya**	<u>ya</u>cht	**yā**zi (duck), j**iā** (home)
	ian	**yan**	Japanese <u>yen</u>	**yān** (cigarette), d**iàn**shì (TV), q**ián** (money)
	iang	**yang**	<u>young</u>	**yáng** (sheep), x**iǎng** (think)
	iao	**yao**	m<u>eow</u>	**yào** (want), x**iǎo** (small), x**iào** (laugh)
	ie	**ye**	<u>ye</u>t	**yě** (also), x**iè** (thank), t**iě** (iron)
	in	**yin**	l<u>in</u>k	j**īn**tiān (today), **yīn** tiān (cloudy sky)
	ing	**ying**	k<u>ing</u>	**Yīng**guó (UK), **Yīng**wén (English)
	iong	**yong**	<u>yü ohng</u>	**yòng** (use), x**ióng** (bear), q**ióng** (poor)
	iou	**you**	<u>yo-yo</u>	**yǒu** (have), **yóu** (swim)
	iu	—		n**iú** (cow), q**iú** (ball)
	o	o	W<u>a</u>l Mart	w**ǒ** (I, me), b**ō**cài (spinach)
	ong	—	<u>wu ohng</u>	h**óng** (red), t**óng**xüé (classmate)
	ueng	**weng**		**wēng** (an old man, a surname)
	ou	ou	h<u>o</u> h<u>o</u> h<u>o</u>	**ǒu** (lotus root), yǐh**òu** (after)
	u	**wu**	owl sound	**wǔ** (five)
	ua	**wa**	<u>wa</u>tt	**wà**zi (socks), diành**uà** (telephone)
	uai	**wai**	<u>why</u>	**wāi** (tilt), k**uài** (fast, quick)
	uan	**wan**	<u>wan</u>d	**wǎn** (evening, night), g**uān** (close)
	uang	**wang**	<u>wan</u>t	**Wáng** (a surname), h**uáng** (yellow)
	uei	**wei**	<u>way</u>	**wéi** (danger, hello)
	ui	—		sh**uí** (who), h**uì** (can, meeting)
	uen	**wen**	<u>wu n</u>	**wén** (language, mosquito)
	un	—		L**ún**dūn (London)

uo	wo	Wal Mart	**wǒ** (I, me), **guó** (country)
ü	yü	French *ü*	**yǘ** (fish)
üan	yüan	yü an	**yüán** (dollar, round)
üe	yüe	yü ay	**yüè** qì (musical instrument), x**üé**xí (study)
ün	yün	yü n	**yǚn** (dizzy), **jǖn**rén (soldier)

2.2.1   Two life-support letters: y and w

The 'y' and 'w' are neither vowels nor consonants, but they play a life-support role when the vowels starting with 'i,' 'u,' and 'ü' need to stand alone. You may find from the above table under the 'Stand Alone' column that 'y' is used when the vowel begins with 'i' or 'ü,' and 'w' is used when the vowel begins with 'u.'

2.3   Consonants

Here we present in table form a summary of all the consonants in Pīnyīn. You may scan it or study it now, but should refer back to it as often as necessary until you can automatically reproduce the correct sounds.

	Pīnyīn	**English Equivalent**	**Examples**
C o n s o n a n t s	b	<u>b</u>urp	**bú** kè qì (don't be a guest = you're welcome)
	d	<u>d</u>irt	**duì** bù qǐ (excuse me), **dú** (read), **duì** (correct), bú **duì** (incorrect)
	f	<u>f</u>irst	**fāngfǎ** (method)
	g	<u>g</u>ird	yí**ge** (one unit of … = a)
	h	<u>h</u>eard	**hǎo** (good), **hén hǎo** (very good)
	j	<u>j</u>eans	**jī** (chicken), **jīntiān** (today), hǎo**jí**le! (excellent!)
	k	<u>k</u>ernel	**kāishǐ** (begin), shàng**kè** (class in session)
	l	<u>l</u>ook	**lǎoshī** (teacher), **lái** (come, start doing …)
	m	<u>m</u>ercy	**méi** wèntí (no problem)
	n	<u>n</u>erd	**nǐ** (you), **nán**rén (man), **nǚ**rén (woman)
	p	<u>p</u>urse	**péngyǒu** (friend)
	q	<u>ch</u>eetah	duì bù **qǐ** (excuse me), **qǐng** (please), **qù** (go)
	t	<u>t</u>erm	míng**tiān** (tomorrow)

	x	<u>chien</u> (Fr. dog)	**xièxie nǐ** (thank you), **bú yòng xiè** (no need to thank = you're welcome), **xiānsheng** (Mr.), **xiáojie** (Ms.)

2.3.1 Two renegades: q and x

The 'q' and 'x' are two consonants whose pronunciations are far from the English norm. Please practice with the provided equivalents.

2.3.2 To 'ü' or not to 'ü'

In Pīnyīn, the vowel 'u' following the letters j, q, x, and y is always pronounced as ü. Some examples are: jú, qù, xū, and yú. Thus a convention for simplicity was created to eliminate the two dots (umlaut) on top of the ü following j, q, x, and y. However, to minimize our learning effort, we continue to use ü throughout the book without following this minor rule. We will still see the two dots showing up for jǘ, qǜ, xǖ, and yǘ throughout the book.

2.3.3 The Gang of Seven

Among the consonants, these are the seven most difficult ones, which even trouble native Chinese speakers! Their pronunciation rules are described below:

Pīnyīn		English Equivalent	Vocabulary Examples
Basic Unit	**Stand Alone**		
c	ci	ca<u>ts</u> (the hi-hat sound in a drum set)	**cì** (stab), **cóng** (from), **cān** (cuisine)
ch	chi		**chī** (eat), **chá** (tea), **chǎomiàn** (fry-noodle)
s	si	<u>s</u>ay (snake noise)	**sì** (4, temple), **sānmíngzhì** (sandwich)
sh	shi		**shì** (be), **shéi** (who), **Shàolín sì** (temple)
z	zi	ki<u>ds</u> (electric shock sound)	**zǐ** (son), **zài** (at, again), **zàijiàn** (good-bye)
zh	zhi		**zhǐ** (paper), **zhīdào** (know), **zhè** (this)
r	ri	<u>z</u>oo (with tongue curled up)	**rì** (sun, day), **Měiguórén** (American)

(Consonants — label in leftmost merged column)

a) An 'i' is appended to each member of the Gang of Seven only when each stands alone as a syllable, such as in 'ci, si, zi, chi, shi, zhi, and ri.' This 'i' *should not* be pronounced as the '<u>ee</u>' in English word '<u>ee</u>l'. Instead, it should sound like the '<u>i</u>' when you pronounce Engl<u>i</u>sh.

b) The 'h' signifies that you need to pronounce in such way: tongue curled up and suspended midway between roof and floor of the mouth; top and bottom teeth should meet; forceful.

c) Use English 'z' sound and the formation illustrated in item (b) to pronounce **r** or **ri** even there is no 'h' in them.

A compact form is presented in the following:

The Gang of Seven		Stand alone as a syllable	
(1) c	**(4) ch**	(1) ci	(4) chi
(2) s	**(5) sh**	(2) si	(5) shi
(3) z	**(6) zh**	(3) zi	(6) zhi
	(7) r		(7) ri

2.4   Positioning the tone marks

We write a Pīnyīn syllable by combining consonant and vowel. The next step is to place a tone mark somewhere on top of the syllable. In the following we have a set of simple rules to put the tone marks properly:

1) Always place a tone mark on top of the following vowels: 'a, e, i, o, u, and ü'.
2) 'a' and 'e' always get the tone mark. For example: dào, lèi,
3) The rightmost vowel gets the tone mark. For example: guó.
4) For the vowel pair 'ou', the 'o' gets the tone mark. For example: yǐhòu.

2.5   Tone changes

Although carrying the same meaning, a word may be pronounced in different tones depending on the tone of the *next* syllable. Linguistically speaking, 'ease of speaking' is the factor that influences the tone changes.

2.5.1   Two 3rd tones in succession

When two 3rd tones are in succession, such as 'hěn hǎo' (very good), you must pronounce the first syllable at 2nd tone, but the tone notation is left unchanged.

2.5.2   bù vs. bú (not)

'bù' changes to 'bú' only if its next syllable is at 4th tone. For example: bú shì.

2.5.3   yī vs. yí vs. yì (one)

'yi' is pronounced at

- 1st tone (**yī**) when it is used to represent a number '1,' as in a telephone number.
- 2nd tone (**yí**) when the next syllable is at 4th tone, such as yídìng (must).
- 4th tone (**yì**), otherwise.

2.6   Pīnyīn tools

Several Pīnyīn-related websites are provided in the following for additional pronunciation help and practice. Although this list is certainly not exhaustive.

a) http://www.pinyin.org

A good site for pronunciation practice.

b) http://www.csulb.edu/~txie/PINYIN/pinyin.htm

You can create Pīnyīn text in Word, but you need to create a macro file in Word 97 or 2000. After you have created a macro file, type the text in Pīnyīn with numbers. Run the macro and the Pīnyīn with numbers will be converted to Pīnyīn with tone marks.

c) http://www.pinyin.info/unicode/marks3.html

Convert tone numbers to tone marks.

d) http://www.zhongwen.com/

Cross search for Chinese words and phrases; a good Chinese dictionary tool.

e) http://www.mandarintools.com

This site provides tools for the people who are already studying and using Chinese.

Direct Correlations
Between English and Chinese

3.1 Direct Correlation: the basic structures

The basic language patterns for English and Chinese are more than just similar, they are correlated. For example, in the 'Subject + Verb + Object/Modifier/Complement' sentence structure shown in **Table 1**, the Chinese and English structures are the same; they 'map' perfectly to each other. Using your rich knowledge of English, an English-Chinese dictionary is sufficient to transform your wealth of 'Subject + Verb + Object/Modifier/Complement' sentences into Chinese for numerous occasions. As a matter of fact, there are many other sentence patterns where these two languages are directly correlated. Before exploring that, let's briefly review some basic English sentence structures.

Basic English sentence structures consist of these elements: Subject, Verb, Object, Modifier, and Complement, as shown below. Surprisingly, so does Chinese!

Subject	Predicate	
Subject	Verb	Object/Modifier/Complement
I	watch	TV (object).
She	drinks	hot (modifier) tea (object).
His friend	is	an English teacher (complement to the Subject).

Let's take a few moments to recall these familiar English terms you've already known for some time.

Subject

Pronouns appear frequently as the subject. In our examples, we will use two types of pronouns: Personal and Demonstrative. Personal Pronouns include: I/me (wǒ), you (nǐ), she/her/he/him/it (tā), we/us (wǒmen), you (nǐmen), and they/them (tāmen). In Chinese, there is no difference between subjective and objective pronouns. For example, 'tā' stands for he, him, she, her, and it, making Chinese easier in terms of word variations. Demonstrative Pronouns include: this (zhège), that (nàge), these (zhèxiē), and those (nàxiē).

Verb

The following four verb groups are frequently encountered while learning Chinese via English.

1) A 'linking verb' is used to link a Subject with its Complement, which refers back to the Subject. The most common linking verb is the verb 'to be': is, am, are, was, were. Others are: appear, become, feel, grow, look, seem, smell, sound, taste, etc. The word or phrase that follows immediately after the linking verb is called a **Subject Complement**.

2) A 'main verb' is the key action word in a sentence. Some examples are: see (kàn), drink (hē), eat (chī), have (yǒu), etc. They can be:

- **Transitive**: A transitive verb addresses an Object. For example, look at the sentence 'I teach English.', the word 'teach' is a transitive verb and English is the object for the transitive verb 'teach.' In **Table 1**, the examples use transitive verbs to include broader applications.

- **Intransitive**: An intransitive verb does not address an Object. For example, the intransitive verb 'blossom' in 'The flowers blossom,' does not have an Object after it.

3) In English, the 'Auxiliary verbs' are the **helping** verbs that help the **main** verbs to form negation, questions, tenses, and voices. The English auxiliary verbs are: be (is, am, are, etc.), can, do, have, may, must, shall, will, etc., and they will be discussed in the chapters for 'Question Sentences' and 'Tenses.' Chinese does not have auxiliary verb functions like those in English. Negation, question, tense, and voice sentences are formed in a much easier way.

4) The 'to + root form verb' such as in 'To teach is to learn,' is called an '**Infinitive.**' To form the Chinese counterpart of an English infinitive, simply remove the 'to.'

Objects, Modifiers, Complements

An **object** is the action recipient of a **main** verb. An object can be a noun, pronoun, or noun phrase.

A **modifier** can be an adjective, which modifies a noun or pronoun. A modifier can also be an adverb, which modifies a verb, adjective, or another adverb. The examples for modifiers are illustrated in Table 3 and 4. Starting from this point, we will use an alternative word **specifier** to indicate modifiers, because 'specifier' makes more sense in many situations.

A **complement** is a noun, adjective word, or phrase that complements the meaning of the Subject or Object of that sentence. Examples are shown in Table 1.

1) Subject Complement: The word or phrase that follows the linking verb to specify the subject is a Subject Complement.
2) Object Complement: The word or phrase that follows the object to specify the object is called an Object Complement.

Let's examine Table 1 to learn more about the direct correlations. In the examples you will see that there is no difference in Chinese in regard to the English verb 'to be': is, am, are, was, and were. You may also notice that the articles 'a' or 'an' are missing, because there is no article corresponding to 'a,' 'an,' or 'the' in Chinese.

You may also use this opportunity to memorize the vocabulary words provided in the examples. It is highly recommended that you incorporate these Chinese words into your daily English conversations (**hybriding**) with Chinese people in order to help you apply and memorize the vocabulary. The ultimate goal is to gradually increase the Chinese portion until the whole line is completely Chinese.

You may also use this opportunity to memorize the vocabulary words provided in the examples. It is highly recommended that you incorporate these Chinese words into your daily English conversations (**hybriding**) with Chinese people in order to help you apply and memorize the vocabulary. The ultimate goal is to gradually increase the Chinese portion until the whole line is completely Chinese.

In the examples you will see that there is no difference in Chinese in regard to the English verb 'to be': is, am, are, was, and were. You may also notice that the articles 'a' or 'an' are missing, because there is no article corresponding to 'a,' 'an,' or 'the' in Chinese.

applying 'Subject + Verb + Object/Complement' sentences for various situations. The next step is to use the Pinyin Tables in Chapter 2 to practice your pronunciation.

CHAPTER 3: DIRECT CORRELATIONS BETWEEN ENGLISH & CHINESE

Table 1: Basic Structures

subject	linking verb 'to be'	subject complement (noun)
I (Wǒ), You (Nǐ), She/He (Tā), We (Wǒmen), You (Nǐmen), They (Tāmen)	is/am/are/was/were	teacher (lǎoshī) / student (xuéshēng) / engineer (gōngchéngshī)
This (Zhège), That (Nàge), These (Zhèxiē), Those (Nàxiē)	(shì)	book (shū) / pen (bǐ) / door (mén), table (zhuōzi) / chair (yǐzi)

subject	main verb	object
I (Wǒ), You (Nǐ), She/He/It (Tā), etc.	eat (chī)	

subject	main verb	object
I (Wǒ), You (Nǐ), She/He (Tā), We (Wǒmen), You (Nǐmen), They (Tāmen)	drink (hē)	coffee (kāfēi) / tea (chá)
	play (dǎ)	ball (qiú)
	have (yǒu)	cat (māo) / gǒu (dog)

subject	main verb	object complement (noun)
The committee (Wěiyuánhuì)	elects (xuǎn)	as (wéi) chairman (zhǔxí)
I (Wǒ)	ask (yào)	him (tā) / to go (qù)
We (Wǒmen)	call (jiào)	Captain Kirk (Kòukè Chuánzhǎng)

It is recommended that the chosen words for a correct sentence in all the tables are sound and related to real-life. Now, let's practice creating our own sentences in the following exercises:

Exercise

subject	linking verb 'to be'	subject complement

subject	main verb	object
1)		

subject	main verb	object
2)		

subject	main verb	object complement
3)		
4)		

---------- **Culture-Specific Note** ----------

CHAPTER 3: DIRECT CORRELATIONS BETWEEN ENGLISH & CHINESE

Many English adjectives and prepositions can be used as 'verbs' in Chinese. Thus, many of these unique Chinese 'verbs' do not have English equivalents. These verbs help to make the sentences shorter and more robust as illustrated below. More examples are provided in §3.7.3.

	English			Chinese		
subject	**'be'**	**adj./prep**	**object**	**subject**	**main verb**	**object**
You	are	good.		Nǐ	hǎo ('good' as verb).	
The teacher	is	in.		Lǎoshī	zài ('in' as verb).	
Mr. Wang	is	at	home.	Wáng xiānsheng	zài ('at' as verb)	jiā.

-------- **End of Note** --------

Because English **adjectives** can also be used as **main verbs** in Chinese to form the basic 'subject + verb' structure, the linking verb 'to be' (shi) is no longer needed in Chinese as shown in the examples below. The only chance for the linking verb 'to be' to survive is if the word(s) following it is a **noun** or **noun phrase**. Refer to §3.7.2 of Culture-Specific Notes at the end of the chapter for examples where the linking verb 'to be' is kept.

English:	She	is	pretty. **(adjective)**		She	is	smart. **(adjective)**
Chinese:	Tā	—	piàoliang. **(main verb)**		Tā	—	cōngmíng. **(main verb)**

English:	I	am	delighted. **(adjective)**		I	am	concerned. **(adjective)**
Chinese:	Wǒ	—	gāoxìng. **(main verb)**		Wǒ	—	dānxīn. **(main verb)**

All this leads to an interesting observation: **"Broken English is perfect Chinese, and broken Chinese is perfect English."** More examples are provided in §3.7.1 of Culture-Specific Notes.

Often, 'very' (hěn) may be added optionally before the main verb for emphatic purpose as shown in the examples below. (Square brackets […] denote the content is optional.)

She	is	pretty. **(adjective)**		She	is	smart. **(adjective)**
Tā	[hěn (very)]	piàoliang. **(main verb)**		Tā	[hěn (very)]	cōngmíng. **(main verb)**
I	am	delighted. **(adjective)**		I	am	concerned. **(adjective)**

Wǒ	[hěn (very)]	gāoxìng. (main verb)	Wǒ	[hěn (very)]	dānxīn. (main verb)

1) Diamond is expensive.	
2) She is nervous.	
3) Your grapes are sour.	
4) I'm careful.	

Answer: 1) Zhuànshí [hěn] guì.   2) Tā [hěn] jǐnzhāng.   3) Nǐde pútao [hěn] suān.   4) Wǒ [hěn] xiǎoxīn.

We often see that the verb 'to be' is omitted in many cases. However, **non-'to be'** linking verbs carry unique meanings and therefore cannot be dropped.

Subject	non-'to be' linking verbs		complement (adjective)
I (Wǒ)	feel (gǎnjué)		comfortable (shūfú).
He (Tā)	seems (sìhū)		happy (gāoxìng).
You (Nǐ)	look (kànqǐlái)	[very (hěn)]	tired (lèi).
It (Tā)	sounds (tīngqǐlái)		high (gāo).

Exercise

1) My boss seems unhappy.	
2) Our business remains promising.	
3) It tastes hot (spicy).	

Answer: 1) Wǒde lǎobǎn sìhū [hěn] bùgāoxìng.   2) Wǒmende shēngyì rénrán [hěn] yǒuxīwàng.   3) Tā cángqǐlái [hěn] là.

3.2 Direct Correlation: to include noun counting

In English, we usually find an article 'a,' 'an,' 'the' precedes a singular noun, such as: I am a teacher. In Chinese, there is no role for the articles 'a,' 'an,' 'the.' However, when it comes to *counting* a noun, a 'measure word' or 'unit' is used as shown in **Table 2**. This is also the way the Chinese language represents its *plural* form. The format is 'Number + Unit + Noun.' For example:

Table 2: To Include Noun Counting

subject	verb	Number	Unit	Noun
I (Wǒ), You (Nǐ), She/He/It (Tā), We (Wǒmen), You (Nǐmen), They (Tāmen)	is / am / are / etc. (shi)	1 (yī)	**ge** (no English counterpart)	teacher (lǎoshī) / student (xuésheng)
	have (yǒu)	2 (liǎng)	**tóu** (head of)	cattle (niú)
	have (yǒu)	3 (sān)	**zhī** (no English counterpart)	cat (māo) / dog (gǒu)
	drink (hē)	…	**bēi** (cups of)	coffee (kāfēi) / tea (chá)
	watch (kàn)		**chǎng** (no English counterpart)	movie (diànyǐng) / ball game (qiú sài)

A list of commonly used unit words are included in Appendix B section §B.11. **Tip:** you may use 'ge' if you cannot remember exactly what unit word to use for a specific noun. The 'unit' word becomes optional (mostly omitted) when you use unspecific 'number' words, such as: several, some, many, a few, etc., as shown in Exercise 4) below.

1) I drank five **cups of** Starbucks coffee.

2) I have two cats and three dogs.

3) I ate two cheeseburgers and three hot dogs.

4) I have several horses.

Answer: 1) Wǒ hē le (le: a past tense tag, see chapter 6) wǔ **bēi** Starbucks kāfēi. 2) Wǒ yǒu liǎng **zhī** māo hé sān **zhī** gǒu. 3) Wǒ chī le liǎng **ge** nǎilàohànbǎo hé sān **ge** rè gǒu. 4) Wǒ yǒu yìxiē mǎ.

3.3 Direct Correlation: to include adjectives

An adjective word, phrase, or clause is used to specify a noun. In English, an adjective sits **before** the noun, while an adjective phrase or clause sits **after** the noun. In Chinese, adjective words, phrases, and clauses all come **before** the noun. Let's take a quick look at these adjective types:

Adjective word

CHAPTER 3: DIRECT CORRELATIONS BETWEEN ENGLISH & CHINESE

Adjective words are those such as: beautiful (měilì), costly (guì), good (hǎo), filthy (āngzāng), serious (yánzhòng), sweet (tián), my (wǒde), your (nǐde), his (tāde), today's (jīntiān de), many (xǔduō), some (yīxiē), any (rènhé), one (yī), two (liǎng), etc. Note that the possessive words such as my, your, his/her, today's, mom's, etc., are also adjectives.

As you see in **Table 3**, following each adjective word or phrase an **adjective indicator 'de'** (的) is inserted, such as: red (hóngsè **de**), today's (jīntiān **de**), very good (hén hǎo **de**), etc. When you look in the dictionary, the '**de**' accompanies those possessive form adjectives, but you must mentally add a '**de**' for other adjectives. Although in **Table 3** we only give examples on **adjective words** to simplify our presentation, we will demonstrate the next two groups of adjectives in Chapter 4 – The Cross Correlations between English & Chinese.

Adjective phrase

- The *dog (n.)* with brown spots (adj. phrase) won the first prize.
- The *vase* on the table is from China.
- There are many *things* waiting for us in the future.
- The *boy* waiting for the bus is my brother.
- The *man* helped by the paramedic survived.

Adjective clause

- For *those (n.)* who are interested in Chinese classes (adj. clause), please sign up with Mrs. Smith.
- The *book* I read is about dinosaurs.
- She is a *person* we love.
- This is the *town* where I grew up.

Note 1: In the case of multiple adjectives in succession, we simply keep all 'de's at their current location. For example: 'A big, juicy, sweet, red apple.' (Yí ge dà de, duōzhī de, tián de, hóngsè de píngguǒ.)

Note 2: When 'two' is used as an adjective, such as in 'two apples,' the word 'two' should be pronounced as 'liǎng.'

Table 3: To Include Adjectives

Subject	Verb	Object, Specifier, Complement			
s.	v.	number	unit	adj. (Specifier)	noun (specifyee)
I (Wǒ), You (Nǐ), etc.	am / are (shì)		ge	your (nǐde) / my (wǒde)	teacher (lǎoshī)
	watch (kàn)	1 (yī)	chǎng	very good (hén hǎo) de	movie (diànyǐng)/ball game (qíú sài)
	drink (hē)	2 (liǎng)	bēi (cups of)	very aromatic (hén xiāng) de	coffee (kāfēi)/tea (chá)
	eat (chī)	3 (sān)	ge	sweet (tián) de	apple (píngguǒ)
	use (yòng)	…	zhī (pieces of)	red (hóngsè) de	pencil (qiānbǐ)
	have (yǒu)		zhī	lovely (kěài) de	cat (māo)/dog (gǒu)

Exercise

1) I bought four beautiful dresses.

2) I saw a great opera.

3) I live in New York City's _China Town._

4) The neighbor's grass is _always_ greener.

Answer: 1) Wǒ mǎi le sì jiàn měilì **de** yīfú.   2) Wǒ kàn le yi chǎng hěnbàng **de** gējù.   3) Wǒ zhù zài Niǔ Yuē Shì **de** Zhōngguó Chéng.   4) Línjū **de** cǎo zǒngshì bǐjiào (more) lǜ (green).

The 'de' routine

We see that the additive '**de**' is appended to each adjective as shown in **Table 3**; however, in dictionary use, note that:

1) For the **possessive** adjectives such as your, my, his, etc., a **de** accompanies the word from your dictionary.

2) For other adjectives, remember to add a **de** after the word you looked up in your dictionary.

Situations where 'de' can be dropped

1) Two nouns in succession

As in English, when two nouns are placed in succession, such as 'sports model', the first word 'sports' functions as an adjective to specify what kind of model is being described. In this case, the '**de**' is dropped, and we have a direct correlation between English and Chinese.

English		less common Chinese	de		common Chinese	
tree	bark	shù	**de**	pí	shù	pí
computer	screen	diànnǎo	**de**	píngmù	diànnǎo	píngmù
car	engine	chēzi	**de**	yǐnqíng	chēzi	yǐnqíng

2) Near and dear

For the **possessive** adjectives, such as your, my, his, and her, the '**de**' can be dropped when the *possessed* noun is considered in Chinese culture as 'near and dear.' A handful of nouns are in this category. These are family members, teachers, classmates, schools, churches, companies, teams, houses, spouses, girlfriends/boyfriends/fiancées, etc.

English	less common Chinese			common Chinese
your wife	nǐ	**de**	tàitai	nǐ tàitai
our school	wǒmen	**de**	xuéxiào	wǒmen xuéxiào
my house	wǒ	**de**	jiā	wǒ jiā

3) Single syllabic Chinese adjective word

English	less common Chinese			common Chinese
good movie	*hǎo*	**de**	diànyǐng	hǎo diànyǐng
sour bread	*suān*	**de**	miànbāo	suān miànbāo
red pencil	*hóng*	**de**	qiānbǐ	hóng qiānbǐ

4) Well-known phrase

English	less common Chinese			common Chinese
general hospital	zǒng	**de**	yīyuàn	zǒng yīyuàn
political science	zhèngzhì	**de**	kēxué	zhèngzhì kēxué
American embassy	Měiguó	**de**	dàshǐguǎn	Měiguó dàshǐguǎn

Possessive form: A of B = B's A = B de A

The possessive form is also an adjective, thus a **de** (的) is required as an adjective indicator. For example, The Wizard of Oz = Oz's Wizard = Oz **de** Wizard; The Dukes of Hazzard = Hazzard's Dukes = Hazzard **de** Dukes.

This is		a leg	of	that table.
Zhè shì		nàge zhuōzi	**de**	yì tiáo (unit) tuǐ.

There is		a garden	in	front	of	the post office.
Yǒu		yíge huāyuán	zài	yóu jú	**de**	qiánmiàn.

Exercise

1) The price of that house is not cheap.

	de	

2) She is one of my best students.

		de	

3) I'm loyal to the brand of that product.

	de	

Answer: 1) Nàge fángzi | **de** | jiàqián | bù piányi.   2) Tā shì | wǒ zuìhǎo de xüésheng | **de** | yíge.   3) Wǒ zhōngshí yú | nàge chǎnpǐng | **de** | páizi.

3.4 Direct Correlation: to include adverbs

An adverb is a **specifier (modifier)** that specifies (modifies) a verb, adjective, or another adverb. In English, an adverb can be placed either **before** or **after** the word to be specified (we will call it a '**specifyee**' for lack of a more convenient word). In Chinese the adverb sits mostly **before** the specifyee.

The following examples show each adverb sitting **before** the <u>verb</u> it specifies. Clearly, Chinese is one-to-one mapped to its English counterpart.

subject	specifier	specifyee	object
	adverb	verb	
I	often	watch	TV.
Wǒ	cháng	kàn	diànshì.
I	also	drink	tea.

CHAPTER 3: DIRECT CORRELATIONS BETWEEN ENGLISH & CHINESE

Wǒ	yě		hē	chá.
I	careful	ly	did	a survey.
Wǒ	xiǎoxīn	**di**	zuò le	yíge diàochá.

The following examples show each adverb sitting **before** the adjective it specifies. Here also Chinese is one-to-one mapped to its English counterpart.

subject	linking v.	specifier adverb	specifyee adjective
He	is	very	smart.
Tā	—	hěn	cōngmíng
Business	was	quite	difficult.
Shēngyì	—	xiāngdāng	kùnnán.
This coin	is	extreme ly	old.
Zhège yìngbì	—	fēicháng **di**	lǎo.

Exercise

1) The child generously shared his toys.

2) The result was unexpectedly satisfactory.

3) Our business is relatively optimistic.

Answer: 1) Nàge háizi dàfāng **di** fēnxiǎng le tāde wánjù. 2) Jiéguǒ yìwài **di** lìngrénmǎnyì. 3) Wǒmen de shēngyì xiāngdāng **di** lèguān.

Table 4 gives an overall picture with examples of where the adverb comes **before** the verb (specifyee). We will discuss in chapter 4 'Cross Correlation' where the adverb may come **after** the specifyee.

Table 4: To Include Adverbs

subject	adverb (specifier)	verb (specifyee)	number	unit	adjective (specifier)		noun (specifyee)
I (Wǒ),	—	am/are (shì)	1 (yī)	ge	your (nǐde)/my (wǒde)		teacher (lǎoshī) .
You (Nǐ),	often (cháng)	watch (kàn)	2 (liǎng)	chǎng	good ([hěn] hǎo)	de	movie (diànyǐng)
etc.	always (lǎo)	drink (hē)	3 (sān)	bēi (cups of)	aromatic ([hěn] xiāng)	de	coffee (kāfēi)

	eat (chī)	...	ge	sweet ([hěn] tián)	de	apple (píngguǒ)
also (yĕ)	use (yòng)		zhī (pieces of)	red (hóngsè)	de	pencil (qiānbǐ)
rarely (hěnshǎo)	have (yǒu)		zhī	lovely (kě'ài)	de	cat (māo)
happily (kuàilè di)						

3.5 Direct Correlation: to include auxiliary verbs and infinitives

Very often in Chinese two or three verbs appear in succession. These patterns are directly correlated with the following three English structures:

1) The first verb is a transitive verb, and the second verb is an infinitive (to + verb) working as the object for the first verb. However, Chinese does not have the form of an infinitive, so the 'to' is dropped.

	main verb	infinitive		the rest
subject	verb $_1$	to	verb $_2$	
I	like	to	watch	cartoons.
Wŏ	xĭhuān	—	kàn	kātōng.

2) The first verb is an auxiliary verb, and the second verb is a verb in its root form. This is a one-to-one mapping!

	auxiliary verb	main verb	the rest
subject	verb $_1$	verb $_2$	
I	will	buy	a sports car.
Wŏ	yào	mǎi	yíge pǎo chē.

3) The first verb is an auxiliary verb, the second verb is a verb in its root form, and the third is a verb in the infinitive form.

	auxiliary verb	main verb	infinitive		the rest
subject	verb $_1$	verb $_2$	to	verb $_3$	
You	may	come	to	pick up	your	tickets.
Nĭ	néng	lái	—	ná	nĭde	piào.

Table 5 shows the application of the two-verb case to form longer sentences.

Table 5: To Include Auxiliary Verbs & Infinitives

subject	verb ₁	verb ₂	number	unit	adjective (specifier)		noun (specifyee)
I (Wǒ), You (Nǐ), etc.	like (xǐhuān) / love (ài),	watch (kàn)		chǎng	horror (kěpà)	de	movie (diànyǐng)
	desire (xiǎng) / want (yào),	drink (hē)	1 (yī)	bēi (cups of)	decaf (wúkāfēiyīn)	de	coffee (kāfēi)
	will, of future determination (yào)	eat (chī)	2 (liǎng)	piàn (slices of)	whole wheat (quán mài)	de	bread (miànbāo)
	will, of probability (huì)	use (yòng)	3 (sān)	zhī (pieces of)	red (hóngsè)	de	pencil (qiānbǐ)
	can, of ability (huì / néng)	play (dǎ)	...	chǎng	intense (jīliè)	de	basket (lán) ball (qiú)
	can, of permission (kěyǐ)	have (yǒu)		zhī	lovely (kěài)	de	cat (māo)

3.6 Direct Correlation: to include negation

Another important element is negation. In English, we use 'is not,' 'do not,' 'have not,' etc., while in Chinese they are 'bù' or 'méi.'

3.6.1 not = bù

1) 'bù' precedes an 'auxiliary verb.'

s.	aux.	negation	main verb	object
I	can / will	**not**	go	there.
Wǒ	*bù*	néng / huì	qù	nàlǐ.

Note that 'do' has no Chinese counterpart, thus we achieve the following result.

	do	not	go	there.
I		**not**	go	there.
Wǒ	*bù*	–	qù	nàlǐ.

This leads to the next point. Note the tone change.

2) 'bù' precedes any 'main verb' except 'have' (to own).

	do	not	eat	fish.
I	do	**not**	eat	fish.
Wǒ	*bù*	–	chī	yú.
I	do	**not**	want	chicken.

Wǒ	bú	–	yào	jǐ.

3) 'be' (shi) is also a type of 'auxiliary verb', so the above rule applies to 'be' as well.

s.	be (aux.)	negation	noun (complement)
I	am	**not**	a teacher.
Wǒ	*bú*	shi	lǎoshī.

The 'be' in the next example is dropped in Chinese because the word 'difficult' becomes the main verb in Chinese.

s.	be (aux.)	negation	adjective (complement)
This problem	is	**not**	difficult.
Zhège wèntí	*bú*	(dropped)	**main verb** kùnnán.

4) In the case of an 'imperative mood' like ordering or commanding, the English **'not'** can be replaced by '**bú yào**' or '**bié**.'

Please		do	not	smoke.
Qǐng	**bú yào**		–	xīyān.

Don't	forget	to bring	money.
Bú yào	wàngjì	dài	qián.

5) '**bù**' changes its tone to '**bú**' only if its next syllable is at 4th tone. For example: bú shì.

6) '**bié**' corresponds to '**bù**' in limited cases. See Chapter 8 for details.

3.6.2 not = méi

'Méi' is used in two applications:

1) **not = méi** and works with the main verb '**have**' to mean 'do not have/own/possess.'

s.		main verb	object
I		**have**	money.
Wǒ		**yǒu**	qián.
I	do not	**have**	money.
Wǒ	*méi* –	**yǒu**	qián.

CHAPTER 3: DIRECT CORRELATIONS BETWEEN ENGLISH & CHINESE

I	do	not	have	a problem.
Wǒ		méi	[yǒu]	wèntí.
We	do	not	have	argument.
Wǒmen		méi	[yǒu]	zhēngzhí.

Exercise

1) We	do	not	have	passports.
2) I	do	not	eat	meat.

Answer: 1) Wǒmen | méi | yǒu | hùzhào.   (2) Wǒ | bù | chī | ròu.

It is conceivable that culture-specific idiomatic usages in English are not applicable to the <u>mapping rules</u>. Therefore, staying with **baseline** English usage is a **must** in using English to learn Chinese.

culture-specific	I		have no		money.
baseline	I	do	not	have	money.
Chinese	Wǒ	méi	—	[yǒu]	qián.
culture-specific	My car		is out of		gas.
baseline	My car	does	not	have	gas.
Chinese	Wǒde chē	méi	—	[yǒu]	qìyóu.

2) méi yǒu

– For negating a past event: **méi yǒu = didn't = 'past tense' not.**
– For negating in a perfect tense: **méi yǒu = not** (see Chapter 6)

	s.	aux.	negation	main verb	**obj.**
(1)	I	do	**not**	eat	breakfast.
(2)	Wǒ	**bù**	–	chī	zǎofàn.
(3)	I	did	**not**	eat	breakfast.
(4)	Wǒ	*méi yǒu*	–	chī	zǎofàn.

Note that the difference between line (1) and (3) is significant, and so are the Chinese lines (2) and (4). Table 6 shows the incorporation of negation into a sentence.

Table 6: Negation

subject	negation	verb 1	verb 2	number	unit	adjective (specifier)	(de)	noun (specifyee)	(end)
Wǒ (I)	**bú (not)**	—	am (shì)		—	nǐde (your)		teacher (lǎoshī)	
Wǒ (I), Nǐ (You), etc.	**bu (do not)**	like (xǐhuān), love (ài), desire (xiǎng), want (yào), will (yào/huì), can (huì), …	watch (kàn)	1 (yí)	chǎng	horror (kěpà)		movie (diànyǐng)	
			drink (hē)	2 (liǎng)	cups of (bēi)	decaf (wúkāfēiyīn)		coffee (kāfēi)	
			eat (chī)	3 (sān)	slices of (piàn)	whole wheat (quán mài)	de	bread (miànbāo)	.
			use (yòng)	…	pieces of (zhī)	red (hóngsè)		pencil (qiānbǐ)	
			play (dǎ)		chǎng	intense (jīliè)		basket (lán) ball (qiú)	
	méi (do not)	—	have (yǒu)		zhī	brown (zōngsè)		cat (māo)	

3.6.3 Positioning of 'adverb' and 'negation' in a sentence

Adverb and negation should typically be placed in the order as shown below.

	subject	negation	adverb	negation	verb 1	verb 2	object
(1)	Wǒ (I)	—	—	**bù**	xǐhuān (like)	chī (eat)	Sushi.
(2)		—	yě (also)	**bù**	xǐhuān (like)		
(3)		—	zuótiān (yesterday)	**méi yǒu**	—		
(4)		**bù**	cháng (often)	**bù**	—		

Note that in line (4) the **bù** can be at either, but not both, places to carry different meanings in English.

3.7 Culture-Specific Notes

Having looked at the direct mapping relationship between English and Chinese, here we turn our attention to several interesting culture-specific aspects of Chinese.

3.7.1 The adjective in 'to be + adjective' turns into 'main verb' in Chinese

The English 'adjective' following the verb 'to be' turns into the 'main verb' in Chinese, as shown in the following examples.

English			Chinese		
subject	verb 'to be'	adjective	subject		main verb
He	is	hungry.	He (Tā)		hungry (è).
She	is	tired.	She (Tā)		tired (lèi).
I	am	cold.	I (Wǒ)		cold (lěng).

3.7.2 The 'shì ... de' Sandwich

There is a unique Chinese structure that uses 'shì ... de' to sandwich the predicate. We use this structure in our conversations to emphasize, confirm, or reiterate a known point.

Case 1) If the verb in the sentence is the verb 'to be' (shì), then only one 'shì' is kept to avoid duplication.

subject	shì	predicate	de.
subject	verb 'to be'	adjective	
She (Tā)	is (shì)	pretty (piàoliang)	
		smart (cōngmíng)	de.
That (Nà)		incorrect (búduì)	
This (Zhège) team (duì)		invincible (wúdí)	

Exercise

	shì		de.
	shì		

1) Grass is green.

2) This apple is red.

3) Your grapes are sour.

Answer: 1) Cǎo | shì | lǜ | de.   2) Zhège píngguǒ **shì** hóng **de**.   3) Nǐde pútao **shì** suān **de**.

subject	shì	predicate	de.
subject	verb 'to be'	adjective	
He/She (Tā)	is (shì)	*from* afar (*cóng yuǎnfāng lái*)	de.

32

This problem (Zhège wèntí)		not difficult (bù nán)

Exercise

1) She is *from* America.	2) His accent is not heavy.

Answer: 1) Tā **shì** *cóng* měiguó *lái* **de.**   2) Tāde kǒuyīn **shì** bú zhòng **de.**

Also note that the subject complement can be converted into an <u>adjective</u> via the '**shì … de**' sandwich as shown below.

subject	shì		predicate	
subject	**verb 'to be'**	**article**	**subject complement (noun)**	**de.**
I (Wǒ)	am (**shì**)	[a (yíge)]	teacher (lǎoshī).	
			adjective	
			v.	**obj.**
I (Wǒ)	am (**shì**)	[a (yíge)]	teach (jiāo)	book (shū)	**de.**

subject	**verb 'to be'**	**article**	**subject complement (noun)**	**de.**
I (Wǒ)	am (**shì**)	[a (yíge)]	doctor (yīshēng).	
			adjective	
			v.	**obj.**
I (Wǒ)	am (**shì**)	[a (yíge)]	see (kàn)	illness (bìng)	**de.**

Exercise

1) I am a software engineer.	**shì**		**de.**
2) I am a pilot.	**shì**		**de.**
3) I am a fisherman.	**shì**		**de.**

Answer: 1) Wǒ **shì** [yíge] xiě ruǎnjiàn **de.**   2) Wǒ **shì** [yíge] kāi fēijī **de.**   3) Wǒ **shì** [yíge] bǔ yú **de.**

Case 2) If the verb in the sentence is a main verb, then '**shì**' is placed right before the main verb. The cross relationship will be explained in Chapter 4.

subject	shi	predicate					de.
		main verb	the rest of the sentence				
I		want	to	become	a	musician.	
Wǒ	shi	xiǎng	—	chéngwéi	[yíge]	yīnyuèjiā	de.
I		came		by train.			
Wǒ	shi	zuò huǒche	lái				de.

Exercise

1) He will come.

	shi						de.

2) She can play piano.

3) She will go to China.

Answer: 1) Tā | shi | huì | lái | de.   2) Tā shi huì tán gāngqíng de.   3) Tā shi yào qù Zhōngguó de.

3.7.3 Popular Chinese main verbs that have no English counterpart

jiào (叫)

	subject	main verb	object	object complement
English:	People	call	me	Adam.
Chinese:	Dàjiā	jiào	wǒ	Yàdāng.

So,

Chinese			English
subject	main verb	object	English
Wǒ	jiào	Yàdāng.	My name is Adam. / I'm Adam.

xìng (姓)

'Xing' is another unique Chinese main verb that has no English counterpart. It is equivalent to using 'surname' as a verb, such as in faulty English 'I surname Smith.' But it is perfect Chinese!

English

CHAPTER 3: DIRECT CORRELATIONS BETWEEN ENGLISH & CHINESE

subject	verb to be	complement	subject	main verb	object	object compl.
My surname	is	Smith	•			
			People	call	me	Adam.

Chinese

subject	main verb	object		main verb	object	
I (Wǒ)	surname (xìng)	Smith (Shǐmìsī)		jiào	Yǎdāng.	

Or equivalently,

subject	main verb	object	
I (Wǒ)	call (jiào)	Shǐmìsī	Yǎdāng.

The question form is:

What is your name?

subject	main verb	inter. adjective	object	
You (Nǐ)	call (jiào)	what (shénme)	name (míngzi)	?

zhǎo (找)

	subject	verb 1	verb 2	object	
English:	I	want (=would like)	to talk to	Mr. Wang.	
			to meet with		
Chinese:	Wǒ	xiǎng	zhǎo	Wáng xiānsheng.	

More 'culture-specific words and phrases' are discussed in Chapter 8.

4

Cross Correlations Between English and Chinese

In both English and Chinese, a **specifier** is a word or phrase that makes what you say more specific. The specifiers are adjective words, adjective phrases, adverb words, and adverb phrases. An adjective specifier specifies a noun or pronoun – the specifyee. An adverb specifier specifies a verb, adjective, or another adverb – the specifyee. When using a specifier, you are able to avoid having the listener ask 'who, what, where, when, why, how, and how many/much' questions. In other words, you may avoid hearing the listener say, "Could you be more specific?"

In English, the specifier can be located either **before** or **after** the specifyee, while in Chinese the specifier *typically* sits **before** the specifyee. This fact is summarized in the following table, which also serves as a guide to the topic sections.

Specifier (Before)	Specifyee	Specifier (After)
English		
Adjective Word (§ 4.1)	• Noun	**Adjective Phrase** (§ 4.2)
Adverb Word (§ 4.3)	• Verb • Adjective • Adverb	**Adverb Word and Phrase** (§ 4.3, § 4.4)
Chinese		
All Adjectives (§ 4.1, § 4.2)	• Noun	—
Most Adverbs (§ 4.3, § 4.4)	• Verb • Adjective • Adverb	**In some cases** (§ 4.3, §4.5)

In the following sections, we will demonstrate that depending on the position of a specifier, the structural relationship between Chinese and English can be either directly correlated (one-to-one mapped) or 'crossly' correlated (backwards or reverse mapped).

4.1 Adjective Words

English adjectives usually come before the noun they specify, and this is also true of Chinese. Let's examine several examples below. Note that following each adjective word or phrase, an **adjective indicator 'de'** (的) is appended. When you look up words in the dictionary, the 'de' accompanies the possessive form adjectives (e.g. your = nǐ**de**), but you must mentally add a 'de' for other adjectives:

	Specifier (adjective)		Specifyee (noun)
I (Wǒ) am (shì)	your (nǐ**de**)		teacher (lǎoshī).
This (Zhè) is (shì) a (yíge)	red (hóngsè)	**de**	apple (píngguǒ).

Exercise		
1) I had a	great (lousy, busy)	weekend.
2) This is a	very good	movie.
3) This is a cup of	very aromatic	coffee.

Answer: 1) Wǒ yǒu yíge │ hěnbàng (bùzěnmeyàng, máng) **de** │ zhōumò.   2) Zhè shì yíge │ hěn hǎo **de** │ diànyǐng.   3) Zhè shì yì bēi │ hěn xiāng **de** │ kāfēi

Tip: Repeating the adjective word adds emphasis.

English	Chinese		Repeated adj.	
red	hóng		hóng hóng	
cold	lěng		lěng lěng	
happy	kuàilè	**de**	kuài kuài lè lè	**de**
clean	gānjìng		gān gān jìng jìng	
clear	qīngchǔ		qīng qīng chǔ chǔ	

4.2   Adjective Phrase

An adjective phrase is a group of words joined together for specifying a noun or a noun phrase. Remember that there is always an adjective indicator '**de**' after each adjective word or phrase.

Specifyee (n.)		Specifier (adj. phrase)	be	pronoun
The book		<u>on</u> the table	is	mine.
Specifier (adj. phrase)		**Specifyee (n.)**		
<u>Zài zhuōzi shàng</u>	**de**	shū	shì	wǒde.

In Chinese, there is no counterpart for English articles 'a,' 'an,' and 'the.' However, if in a sentence, the word 'the' works as an **adjective** 'this' or 'that,' use '**zhège**' for 'this' and '**nàge**' for 'that'; otherwise, just ignore it. When 'this' is used as a **pronoun,** such as in sentence, "This is my friend," the Chinese counterpart for 'this' is '**zhè**.'

Exercise			
1) The vase		on the table	<u>came from</u> China.
	de		
2) The car		under the tree	is mine.
	de		
3) The boy		who <u>is taking pictures</u>	is my son.
	de		

Answer: 1) Zài zhuōzi shàng │ de │ huāpíng │ <u>lái zì</u> Zhōngguó.   2) Zài shù xià │ de │ chēzi │ shì wǒde.   3) <u>Zài zhàoxiàng</u> │ de │ nánhái shì wǒde érzi. (Note: English relative pronouns, such as who, that, which, where, etc., have no Chinese counterparts.)

		Specifyee (n.)	Specifier (adj. phrase)
English:	He is a	man	of courage.
		Specifier (adj. phrase)	**Specifyee (n.)**
Chinese:	Tā shì yīge	yǒu yǒngqì	de │ rén.

Exercise			
1) He is a		man	of action.
	yǒu	**de**	

2) He is a	man		with integrity (honesty/of honor).
	yǒu	**de**	
3) She is a	person		we all love.
		de	

Answer: 1) Tā shì yíge │ yǒu xíngdòng │ **de** │ rén.   2) Tā shì yíge │ yǒu chéngshí │ **de** │ rén.
3) Tā shì yíge │ wǒmen dōu ài │ **de** │ rén.

4.3 Adverb Word

Remember that the function of an adverb word or phrase is to specify a verb, adjective, or another adverb word or phrase. There are several kinds of adverbs in English:

The **adverb of**

a) **Manner**: well, fast, slow, hard, early, badly, quickly, slowly, carefully, happily, etc.

b) **Time**: today, next week, before, last night, etc.

c) **Frequency**: always, usually, rarely, seldom, never, once a year, etc.

d) **Degree**: very, much, almost, too, so, enough, etc.

e) **Place**: here, there, behind, everywhere, upstairs, above, etc.

We will use the following sections to demonstrate the correlative relationship between Chinese and English.

4.3.1 Adverb of Manner

The adverbs in this group are words such as quickly, slowly, carefully, easily, happily, beautifully, confidently, well, fast, slow, hard, early, late, loud, fine, etc. Some sit either **before** or **after** the specifyee, and some sit only **after** the specifyee:

(1) Sitting at either <u>before</u> or <u>after</u> the specifyee

Adverb words with this characteristic are generally in a format like: adj. + ly, for example, careful + 'ly.' The additive '**di**' (地) can be considered as the English suffix 'ly.' We may easily find that the 'before' case is directly correlated, the 'after' case is crossly correlated, and the Chinese end results are the same because Chinese requires the specifier to always sit 'before' the specifyee.

Before

s.	specifier (adv.)		specifyee (v.)	object
We	careful	ly	finished	this project.
Wǒmen	xiǎoxīn	**di**	wánchéng le	zhège xiàngmù.

After

s.	specifyee (v.)	object	specifier (adv.)
We	finished	this project	carefully.
	Specifier (adv.)	**specifyee (v.)**	**object**
Wǒmen	xiǎoxīn **di**	wánchéng le	zhège xiàngmù.

<table>
<tr><td colspan="5">Exercise</td></tr>
<tr><td>1) We</td><td>carefully</td><td></td><td>conducted</td><td>a survey.</td></tr>
<tr><td></td><td></td><td>di</td><td></td><td></td></tr>
<tr><td>2) He</td><td>unintentionally</td><td></td><td>tripped</td><td>me.</td></tr>
<tr><td></td><td></td><td>di</td><td></td><td></td></tr>
<tr><td colspan="3">3) He went home happily.</td><td colspan="2">4) She sings happily.</td></tr>
<tr><td colspan="3"></td><td colspan="2"></td></tr>
</table>

Answer: 1) Wŏmen│xiǎoxīn│**di**│zuò le│yíge diàochá.   2) Tā│wúxīn│**di**│bàndǎo le│wŏ. Note that 'le' is a past tense tag to be discussed in Chapter 6.   3) Tā gāoxìng **di** huí jiā le.   4) Tā gāoxìng **di** chàng.

(2) Sitting only <u>after</u> the specifyee

In English, some Manner Adverbs, such as fast, hard, well, late, etc., show up only **after** the verb, to describe the 'result' of the verb action. Interestingly, in Chinese, a **de (得)** is used to introduce the 'result' (in adjective form) for the verb. The **de** combines with the 'result' adjective to form an adverb for specifying the specifyee – verb. Consequently, it forms a direct correlative relationship with its English counterpart, as demonstrated below. **De** takes the neutral tone.

		specifyee	specifier	
English	subject	verb	result adverb	
Chinese	subject	verb	de	result adjective

English	He	plays	well / bad.		I	get up	early.	
Chinese	Tā	dǎ	**de**	hǎo / bùhǎo.	Wǒ	qǐ	**de**	zǎo.

English	I	study	hard.		You	speak	fast / slow.	
Chinese	Wǒ	xüéxí	**de**	rènzhēn.	Nǐ	shuō	**de**	kuài / màn.

English	He	arrived	late.		He	speaks	fluently.	
Chinese	Tā	dào	**de**	chí.	Tā	shuō	**de**	liúlì.

Note the structure in previous section 'fluently = fluent+ly (**di**)' also works. For example, 'He fluently speaks.' (Tā liúlì **di** shuō.)

<table>
<tr><td colspan="6">Exercise</td></tr>
<tr><td>1) My garden</td><td>grows</td><td>well.</td><td>3) She</td><td>sleeps</td><td>late.</td></tr>
<tr><td></td><td>de</td><td></td><td></td><td>de</td><td></td></tr>
<tr><td>2) He</td><td>jumps</td><td>high.</td><td>4) My hair</td><td>*was* cut</td><td>too short.</td></tr>
<tr><td></td><td>de</td><td></td><td></td><td>de</td><td></td></tr>
</table>

Answer: 1) Wǒde huāyüán | zhǎng | **de** | hǎo.　2) Tā | tiào | **de** | gāo.　3) Tā | shuì | **de** | wǎn.　4) Wǒde tóufa | _bèi_ jiǎn | **de** | tài duǎn [le].

Continuing the above, if the verb addresses an object, then we simply place the object right after the subject, and the rest stay the same.

s.		v.	obj.	adv.	
He		studies	_Chinese_	hard.	
Tā	_Zhōngwén_	xuéxí		**de**	rènzhēn.
You		speak	_Chinese_	well/fast.	
Nǐ	_Zhōngwén_	shuō		**de**	hǎo/kuài.
He		plays	_basketball_	well.	
Tā	_lánqiú_	dǎ		**de**	hǎo.

Exercise

1) He		writes	software	well.	
				de	
2) She		designs	hardware	quickly.	
				de	
3) She		tests	the product	laboriously.	
				de	
4) He		excels at		writing software.	

Answer: 1) Tā | ruǎnjiàn | xiě | **de** | hǎo.　2) Tā | yìngjiàn | shèjì | **de** | kuài.　3) Tā | chǎnpǐn | chèshì | **de** | nǔlì.　4) Tā | shàncháng zài | xiě ruǎnjiàn. (Alert! This one has a different structure where 'writing software' is a noun phrase, not an adverb.)

The following example illustrates the 'negation' case:

	I	didn't	sleep	well		last night.
Zuó wǎn (Last night)	wǒ	méiyǒu	suì	[de]	hǎo.	
Zuó wǎn (Last night)	wǒ	—	suì	[de]	bù hǎo.	

Refer to §4.5 Culture-Specific Notes at the end of this chapter for more examples where the specifier comes after the specifyee.

4.3.2　Adverb of Time

These are words such as today, next week, before, last night, etc. The rule for this case is to place the **time adverb** at the beginning of the sentence the same way as in English, or immediately after the subject.

	s.	v.	object	Time Adverb
	I	will go to	China	_tomorrow._
Time Adverb				

Míngtiān	Wǒ	yào qù	Zhōngguó.	

or

s.	Time Adverb	v.	object	
Wǒ	*míngtiān*	yào qù	Zhōngguó.	

Exercise				
	s.	v.	adv.	Time Adverb
	I	didn't sleep	well	last night.
Time Adverb	s.	v.	adv.	
1)				

s.	Time Adverb	v.	adv.	
2)				

Answer: 1) Zuó wǎn │ wǒ │ méiyǒu suì │ [de] hǎo.   2) Wǒ │ zuó wǎn │ méiyǒu suì │ [de] hǎo.

4.3.3 Adverb of Frequency

These are words such as again, always, usually, rarely, often, seldom, never, once a year, etc. Its usage is quite similar to **Adverb of Time**, where in Chinese, it comes directly after the subject or at the beginning of a sentence.

	v.	object	frequency adverb
English	See	you	again.
	specifier (frequency adverb)	specifyee (v.)	object
Chinese	Zài (again)	jiàn (see)	~~nǐ (you)~~. (dropped in Chinese)

Exercise						
1) We	often	go for a walk .		2) Come	again.	

3) I	seldom	travel	*alone* (adv. specifies v. 'travel').	

Answer: 1) Wǒmen │ jīngcháng │ [qù] sànbù.   2) Zài │ lái.   3) Wǒ │ hěnshǎo │ *dāndú* │ lǚxíng.

	s.	v.	object	Frequency Adverb
	I	go to	China	once every two years.
		Frequency Adverb	v.	object
	Wǒ	měi liǎng nián yícì	qù	Zhōngguó.
Frequency Adverb				
Měi liǎng nián yícì	wǒ		qù	Zhōngguó.
Měi liǎng nián	wǒ		qù	Zhōngguó yícì.

Exercise	
1) I play golf once in a while (occasionally).	2) I go to church sometimes.

Answer: 1) Wǒ <u>ǒu'ěr</u> dǎ *gāoěrfū.* 2) Wǒ <u>yǒushí</u> qù jiàotáng.

4.3.4 Adverb of Degree

In English, the 'adverb of degree' is a specifier <u>usually</u> placed **before** the specifyee, forming a direct correlation with its Chinese counterpart. These are words such as really, quite, enough, very, much, almost, too, so, etc. However, 'enough', 'too', and 'as well' always sit at the <u>end</u> of a sentence, forming cross correlation.

s.	v.	specifier adv. of degree	specifyee adj.
The movie	was	really	good.
Zhège diànyǐng	~~shì~~	zhēn	hǎo.

specifyee adj.	specifier adv. of degree
Good	enough.
specifier	*specifyee*
Gòu	hǎo [le]. (le: emphatic)

s.	specifyee v.	obj.	specifier adv. of degree
I	love	you	too.
	specifier	*specifyee*	obj.
Wǒ	yě	ài	nǐ.

Exercise			
s.	specifier adv. of degree	specifyee v.	the rest
1) A deer	almost	hit	my car.
2) I don't	quite	agree with	him.
3)	Enough,		thanks.

Answer: 1) Yìzhī lù | jīhū | zhuàng le | wǒde chē. 2) Wǒ bù | wánquán | tóngyì | tā. 3) Gòu le, xièxie.

4.3.5 Adverb of Place

Some examples of Adverb of Place are: everywhere, elsewhere, forward, here, there, upstairs, up, down, etc. They are placed **after** the verb to describe 'where' the verb takes place.

s.	specifyee v.	specifier adv.
I	looked	everywhere.
	specifier	*specifyee*
Wǒ	dàochù	kàn/zhǎo le.

		specifyee		specifier
s.		v.		adv.
Please	move			forward.
		specifier		specifyee
Qǐng	xiàngqián			yídòng.

Exercise				
I	also looked			*elsewhere (other places).*

Answer: Wǒ | *qítā de dìfāng* | yě kàn/zhǎo le.

The following 'adverb of place' words are in direct correlation with Chinese even though the specifier is **after** the specifyee.

	specifyee	specifier		specifyee	specifier
s.	v.	adv. of place	s.	v.	adv. of place
I	live	here.	He	went	upstairs.
Wǒ	zhù[zài]	zhèlǐ.	Tā	qù le	lóushàng.

Please	sit	down.	Please	stand	up.
Qǐng	zuò	xià.	Qǐng	zhàn	qǐlái.

Exercise					
1) He	left	home.	2) Please	go	away.

Answer: 1) Tā | líkāi le | jiā.   2) Qǐng | zǒu | kāi.

4.4   Adverb Phrase

The adverb phrase **specifier** is used to specify verb, adjective, or adverb **specifyees**. In English, the adverb phrase usually is positioned **after** the specifyee. The most popular adverb phrase is a phrase led by a preposition, i.e. the prepositional phrase, such as: in one week, by Friday, on E-Bay, on the table, in the garden, etc.. The adverb phrases in the following examples are to specify the main verbs: fix, complete, and need, respectively.

	s.	aux.	specifyee (v.)	obj.	specifier (adverb phrase)
Don't worry,	we	will	fix	him	in the parking lot.
	s.	v.	specifier (adverb phrase)	specifyee (v.)	obj.
Búyào dānxīn,	wǒmen	huì	zài tíngchē chǎng lǐ	xiūlǐ	tā.

s.	aux.	specifyee (v.)	obj.	specifier (adverb phrase)
I	will	complete	my plan	in one week.
s.	v.	specifier (adverb phrase)	specifyee (v.)	obj.
Wǒ	yào	zài yíge xīngqī lǐ	wánchéng	wǒde jìhuà.

s.	specifyee (v.)	obj.	specifier (adverb phrase)
I	need	it	by Friday.

s.	specifier (adverb phrase)	specifyee (v.)	obj.
Wǒ	zài xīngqīwǔ yǐqián	xūyào	tā.

Exercise

	s.	specifyee (v.)	obj.	specifier (adverb phrase)
1)	I	buy	stuff	on E-Bay.

	s.	specifyee (v.)	obj.	specifier (adverb phrase)
2) We will		complete	the project	by 6pm today.

Answer: 1) Wǒ | **zài** E-Bay **shàng** | mǎi | dōngxi.   2) Wǒmen yào | **zài** jīngtiān *xiàwǔ* liù diǎn **yǐqián** | wánchéng | zhège xiàngmù.

4.4.1 Prepositional Phrase

A prepositional phrase may function as an **adjective phrase** or **adverb phrase**. Although the prepositions in English are in single word form, their Chinese counterparts are mostly in 'sandwich' format as shown in the following:

Prepositional Phrase				
English		**Chinese**		
Preposition	*Object*	**Left side**	*Object*	**Right side**
above (on top of)	*place*	**zài**	*place*	**shàng[miàn]**
after	*time*	**zài**	*time*	**zhīhòu**
after	*phrase*	—	*phrase*	**zhīhòu**
among	*people, things*	**zài**	*people, things*	**lǐ/zhōng**
among	*classmates*	—	*class* (**bān**)	**shàng**
around	*time*	**zài**	*time*	**zuǒyòu**
as	*role*	**wéi**	*role*	—
at	*place*	**zài**	*place*	—
at / on	*time, dates*	**zài**	*time*	**de shíhòu**
before	*place, people*	**zài**	*place*	**qiánmiàn**
before	*time*	**zài**	*time*	**yǐqián**
behind	*place*	**zài**	*place*	**hòumiàn**
below	*place*	**zài**	*place*	**[yǐ]xià**
beneath	*place*	**zài**	*place*	**xiàmiàn**
beside	*place*	**zài**	*place*	**pángbiān**
besides	*something*	**chúle**	*something*	**yǐwài**
between	*A and B*	**zài**	*A hé B*	**[de] zhōngjiān**
by	*(before) a time point*	**zài**	*time point*	**yǐqián**
by	*(stop at) a time point*	**dào**	*time point*	**wéizhǐ**
by	*place*	**zài**	*place*	**pángbiān**

by	*transportation*	**zuò**	*transportation*	—
during	*activity*	**zài**	*activity*	**de**	**shíhòu/qíjiān**
for (on behalf of)	*people*	**tì**	*people*	—
for	*people, government,...*	**wèi**	*people, government,...*	—
for	*reason*	**wèi le**	*reason*	—
for	*time period*	**yǒu**	*time period*	**[zhījiǔ]**
from	*place*	**cóng**	*place*	—
come from	*place*	**cóng**	*place*	**lái**
	place	**lái zì**	*place*	—
<u>from</u> *point A* <u>to</u> *point B* (time or place)		<u>cóng</u> *point A* <u>dào</u> *point B*		
in	*time period*	**zài**	*time period*	**lǐ**
in	*room, car, place*	**zài**	*room, car, place*	**lǐ**
in	*substance (water, ...)*	**zài**	*substance (water, ...)*	**lǐ**
in	*heart, hand, ...*	**zài**	*heart, hand, ...*	**lǐ/zhōng**
in	*the world*	**zài**	*world*	**shàng**
in	*chair, bed*	**zài**	*chair, bed*	**shàng**
in	*city, country, ...*	**zài**	*city, country, ...*	—
in	*certain aspect*	**zài**	*aspect*	**fāngmiàn**
inside	*place*	**zài**	*place*	**lǐ[miàn]**
into	*place*	**jìn**	*place*	**lǐ**
like	*someone, something*	**xiàng**	*someone, something*	**yíyàng**
near	*place*	**zài**	*place*	**fùjìn**
of	*courage, action,...*	**yǒu**	*courage, action,...*	—
on	*place*	**zài**	*place*	**shàng[miàn]**
opposite to	*place*	**zài**	*place*	**duìmiàn**
outside	*place*	**zài**	*place*	**wàimiàn**
over	*place*	**zài**	*place*	**[zhī]shàng**
past	*time*	**guò**	*time*	—
since	*time*	**zìcóng**	*time*	**[yǐlái]**
till	*time*	**zhídào**	*time*	—
until	*condition*	**zhídào**	*condition*	**wéizhǐ**
to / go to	*place*	**qù**	*place*	—
to	*here*	**dào**	*here*	**lái**
to	*there*	**dào**	*there*	**qù**
toward	*person*	**duì**	*person*	—
toward	*direction*	**wǎng/xiàng**	*direction*	**zǒu**
under	*place*	**zài**	*place*	**xià**
until	*a time point*	**zhídào**	*a time point*	**wéizhǐ**
with	*an aspect*	**zài**	*aspect*	**fāngmiàn**
with (together)	*people*	**hé / gēn**	*people*	**yìqǐ**
with (use)	*tool, material,*	**yòng**	*tool*	—
with (have)	*courage, action, ...*	**yǒu**	*courage, action,...*	—
within	*anything*	**zài**	*anything*	**lǐ / nèi**

Those listed in the table above are frequently used prepositions, but are by no means exhaustive. You may refer to a dictionary or reference books for other cases.

Exercise	
1) I *have lived in* Boston **since** 2002.	
2) He hit me **with a book**.	
3) Sorry, I must leave **at** 2:30.	
4) A smile appeared **on** her face.	
5) You don't love me **at** all!	
6) May I speak to Mr. Wang **of** room 826?	

Answer: 1) Wǒ **zìcóng** 2002 nián **yǐlái** *yǐjīng zhù zài* Boston le.   2) Tā **yòng** shū dǎ [le] wǒ. 3) Duìbùqǐ, wǒ bìxū **zài** liǎng diǎn bàn **[de shíhòu]** líkāi.   4) [Yíge] Wēixiào **zài** tāde lian **shàng** xiǎnchū le.   5) Nǐ **gēnběn** bú ài wǒ!   6) Wǒ néng **gēn** 826 hào fáng **de** Wáng xiānsheng jiǎnghuà (speak) ma?

We are now to observe and appreciate another interesting correlative case between English and Chinese by examining the following examples. In the first sentence, the specifier 'in the water' is to specify where the specifyee 'threw' is happening. However, in the second sentence, the preposition word 'into' belongs to the intransitive verb 'threw' and cannot be used with 'the water' to form an adverb phrase. Therefore, the end result of sentence (2) is a direct correlation. The main point to stress here is that the mapping between English and Chinese is not only on a mechanical level, but also on literal level.

	s.	specifyee (v.)	obj.	specifier (adverb phrase)	
(1)	I	threw	a ball	**in** the *water*.	

	s.	specifier (adverb phrase)	specifyee (v.)	obj.	
	Wǒ	**zài** *suǐ* **lǐ**	diū	qiú.	

	s.	v.	obj.	preposition	obj.
(2)	I	threw	a ball	**into**	the *water*.
	Wǒ	diū	qiú	**jìn** *suǐ* **lǐ**	

Exercise	
My ice cream fell **on** the *floor*.	Note: 'on' belongs to the intransitive verb 'fell'.

Answer: Wǒde bīng qílín diào (fall) **zài** *dìbǎn* **shàng**. (The meaning of past tense 'fell' can be implicit in Chinese. Tense is covered in Chapter 6.)

4.5 Culture-Specific Notes

More examples of 'specifyee + specifier' are provided in this section.

The Initiate-Result Pair

Initiate-result pair is a common Chinese usage that consists of an '**initiating** element' and a '**result** element' to describe the outcome of the '**initiating** element'. The following table summarizes the combinations of the various elements. You will find that if the 'result' is an adverb, then 'de (得)' is not needed to make the sentence work.

Initiate-Result Pair			
Initiating	**Result**	Examples are in	Need 'de (得)' to work?
Verb	**Adverb**	§ 4.5.1	No
	Adjective	§ 4.5.2	Yes
	Verb	§ 4.5.3	Yes
Adjective	**Adjective**	§ 4.5.4	Yes
	Adverb	§ 4.5.5	No

4.5.1   Initiating Verb + Result Adverb

In this case, the <u>initiating verb</u> and <u>result adverb</u> together form a 'verb phrase' serving the verb function as shown in the following examples.

specifyee initiating v.	specifier result adv.	examples
verb phrase		
chī (eat)	bǎo (full, enough)	Nǐ **chī bǎo** le ma? (Did you have enough stuff to eat?)
kàn (see/watch/look)		Nǐ **kàn bǎo** le ma? (Did you have enough stuff to see?)
wán (play)		Nǐ **wán bǎo** le ma? (Did you have enough stuff to play?)
gǎo (do)	cuò (wrong)	Duì bù qǐ, wǒ **gǎo cuò** le. (Sorry, I made a mistake.)
zǒu (walk/travel)		Wǒmen **zǒu cuò** le. (We took a wrong road.)
xiě (write)		Wǒ **xiě cuò** le. (I misprinted.)
suàn (calculate)		Nǐ **suàn cuò** le ba. (You may have miscalculated.)
mǎi (buy)		Wǒ **mǎi cuò** le shū. (I bought the wrong book.)
diū (throw)	diào (vanish)	Tā bǎ tāde qiánbāo **diū diào** le. (He lost his wallet.)
pǎo (run)		Bié ràng nàzhī māo **pǎo diào** le. (Don't let the cat run away.)
shāo (burn)		Yě huǒ **shāo diào** le tāde fángzi. (Wild fire burned down his house.)
sòng (give)		Tā bǎ tāde gǒu **sòng diào** le. (He gave away his dog.)
wàng (forget)		Wǒ bǎ tāde míngzi **wàng diào** le. (I forgot his name.)
tīng (listen)	dǒng (understand)	Nǐ **tīng dǒng** le ma? (Did you understand?)
kàn (read)		Nǐ **kàn dǒng** le ma? (Did you understand?)
zǒu (walk)	hǎo (well)	Qǐng **zǒu hǎo**. (Please walk carefully.)
jiǎng/shuō (talk)		Wǒmen **jiǎng hǎo** le yìqǐ qù chīfàn. (We made an appointment (agreement) to go eat together.)
tīng (listen)	jiàn/dào (reach the target)	Nǐ **tīng jiàn** le ma? (Did you hear it?)
kàn (see/watch/look)		Nǐ **kàn jiàn** le ma? (Did you see it?)

xiào (laugh)	sǐ (to death)	**Xiào sǐ** rén (people) le! (So funny! / Ridiculous!)
qì (angry/mad)		**Qì sǐ** wǒ le! (It got me so angry/mad!)
Any verb that can be finished	wán/hǎo (finish)	Nǐ **chī wán** le ma? (Have you finished eating?)
jì (memorize)	zhù (still)	Wǒ **jì zhù** le tāde míngzi. (I memorized his name.)
tíng (stop)		Qǐng bǎ yīnyuè **tíng zhù**. (Please stop the music.)
kǎ (stuck/jamed)		Jīqì **kǎ zhù** le. (The machine is stuck/jamed.)
zhàn (stand)		**Zhàn zhù!** (Freeze!)
hē (drink)	zuì (drunk)	Nǐ **hē zuì** le. (You are drunk.)
pá (climb)	shàngqù (up there)	Qǐng **pá shàngqù**. (Please climb up there.)
xiě (write)	xiàlái (down)	Qǐng **xiě xiàlái** nǐde dizhǐ. (Please write down your address.)
zǒu (walk)	jìnqù (in there)	Qǐng **zǒu jìnqù**. (Please walk in there.)
pǎo (run)	chūlái (out of)	Qǐng kuài **pǎo chūlái**. (Please quickly run out of there.)
zhàn (stand)	qǐlái (rise up)	Qǐng **zhàn qǐlái**. (Please stand up.)

This table is by no means exhaustive. You may look in a dictionary or other reference books for other cases. The following examples show the case of two adverbs in succession. The 'adv₂' specifies the 'result adv₁,' and the 'result adv₁' specifies the 'initiating verb.'

	specifyee	specifier/specifyee	specifier	
	initiating v.	result adv ₁	adv ₂	**English**
Qǐng (Please)	yí (move)	guòqù (over)	yìdiǎnr (a little).	Please move over a little.
	shuō (speak)	dàshēng (aloud)	yìdiǎnr (a little).	Please speak a little louder.

The following is an exception where it does need 'de' (得) to work. In this very culture-specific case, the adverb word 'hěn' (very) must work with a 'de.'

	specifyee (v.)	specifier (adv.)		
s.	initiating v.	de (得)	result adv.	**English**
Tiānqì (The weather)	lěng (cold)	de	hěn (very).	The weather is <u>very</u> cold.
Kǎoshì (The test)	nán (difficult)			The test was <u>very</u> difficult.

4.5.2 Initiating Verb + Result Adjective

In this case, the 'result adjective' works with 'de' (得) to become an 'adverb specifier' to specify the 'initiating verb.'

	specifyee (v.)	specifier (adv.)		
subject	initiating v.	de (得)	neg.	result adj.
Wǒ	tiào (jump)	de	—	gāo (high).
		[de]	bù	
English: I can (/cannot) jump high.				
Wǒ	chā (wipe)	de	—	gānjìng (clean).
		[de]	bù	

English: I can (/cannot) wipe it clean.				
Wǒde Zhōngwén	shuō (speak)	**de**	—	hǎo (good).
		[de]	bù	
English: My Chinese is (/is not) good.				
Wǒde gǎnmào	hǎo (recover)	**de**	—	duō (more)1e. (le: emphatic)
		[de]	bù	duō (more).
English: My cold is (/is not) much better (Chinese: more recover).				
Tāde fángzi <u>bǐ</u> wǒde fángzi	dà (big)	**de**	—	duō (more).
		[de]	bù	duō (more).
English: His house <u>compares to</u> my house is (/is not) much bigger (Chinese: more big).				

4.5.3   Initiating Verb + Result Verb

In this case, the 'result verb' works with 'de' (得) to become the 'adverb specifier' to specify the 'initiating verb'.

	specifyee (v.)	specifier (adv.)		
subject	**initiating v.**	**de (得)**	**neg.**	**result v.**
Wǒ	tīng (listen)	**de**	—	dǒng (understand).
		—	bù	
English: I [listen and I] can/cannot understand.				
Wǒ	kàn (read)	**de**	—	dǒng (understand).
		—	bù	
English: I [read and I] can/cannot understand.				
Wǒ	kàn (see)	**de**	—	jiàn/dào (reach to the target).
		—	bú	
English: I [see and I] can/cannot find the target.				
Wǒ	zǒu (walk)	**de**	—	dòng (move).
		—	bú	
English: I [walk and I] can/cannot move.				
Wǒ	zhàn (stand)	**de**	—	qǐlái (rise up).
		—	bù	
English: I [stand and I] can/cannot rise up.				
Wǒ	pá (climb)	**de**	—	shàngqù (go up).
		—	bú	
English: I [climb and I] can/cannot climb up.				
Wǒ	chī (eat)	**de**	—	wán (complete).
		—	bù	
English: I [eat and I] can/cannot finish the food.				
Wǒ	mǎi (buy)	**de**	—	qǐ (afford).
		—	bù	
English: I [buy and I] can/cannot afford.				
Wǒ	lái (come)	**de**	—	jí (in time).
		—	bù	
English: I can/cannot make it. (Chinese idiom)				
Tā	kàn (look)	**de**	—	qǐ (up to) wǒ (me).
		—	bù	
English: He looks <u>up to</u> / <u>down upon</u> me. (idiom)				

The following two applications are chiefly used in phrases instead of sentences.

4.5.4   Initiating Adjective + Result Adjective

In this case, the result adjective works with 'de (得)' to specify the initiating adjective.

Specifyee (adj.)	specifier (adv.)		English
initiating adj.	de	result adj.	English
Hǎo (good)			Excellent/Awesome!
Guì (expensive)	de	bù dé liǎo (extreme)!	Too expensive!
Hǎochī (delicious)			Heavenly! Delicious!
Huài / Zāogāo (bad)			Terrible!

4.5.5   Initiating Adjective + Result Adverb

Specifyee (adj.)	specifier (adv.)		English
initiating adj.	result adv.	emphatic tag	English
Hǎo (good)			Excellent/Awesome!
Guì (expensive)	jí (extremely)	le!	Too expensive!
Hǎochī (delicious)			Heavenly delicious!
Huài / Zāogāo (bad)	tòu (extremely)	le!	Terrible!

5

The Question Sentences

Have you noticed that maybe half of your daily conversations with people are questions? Yes, after we have learned in the previous chapters about how Chinese *statement* sentence structures are correlated with that of English, now we are going to examine how they are correlated in *question* sentence structures.

How are questions asked?

The major difference between the two languages is that in English, the question sentences always start with (1) the verb 'to be' or (2) an auxiliary verb such as Do, Can, Have, etc. or (3) an interrogative word such as Who, What, Which, Whose, Where, etc. In Chinese, on the contrary, the subject always leads the sentence and is followed by (1) a question phrase/word or (2) an interrogative word or (3) a question tag at the end of the sentence, as illustrated in the following examples.

English			
verb 'to be'	subject	complement	
Are	you	a teacher	?
Chinese			
subject	verb 'to be'	complement	question tags
Nǐ	shì	lǎoshī	ma?
subject	question phrase	complement	
Nǐ	shì bú shì	lǎoshī	?

English			
interrogative word	verb 'to be'	subject	
Who	are	you	?
Chinese			
subject	verb 'to be'	interrogative word	
Nǐ	shì	shéi	?

Chinese question structures

The following are three ways to compose questions in Chinese:

(1) Although the Chinese language does not use a verb 'to be' or an auxiliary verb to start off a question sentence, it does use them along with a 'true not true' logic to form **question phrases**, such as the 'be not be,' 'auxiliary verb not auxiliary verb,' and 'verb not verb' format.

(2) Similar to English, Chinese also uses **interrogative words**, such as Who, What, Which, Whose, Where, etc..

(3) Chinese uses a **question tag** to pad the end of a statement sentence to form a question. Typical question tags are: ma? ba? ne? méi yǒu? hǎo ma? hǎo bù hǎo?, etc.

We have included a rich set of examples in this chapter to assist you to master these question composing skills. Once this foundation is built, and with the help of a Chinese dictionary for vocabulary, you'll be surprised at how your question speaking and listening abilities will advance.

5.1   The question tags

5.1.1 ma?

Appending a 'ma?' to an affirmative statement constitutes a Chinese question. Let's examine, for example, the popular Chinese greeting line, 'Nǐ hǎo ma?' The word 'Nǐ' is the subject meaning 'You,' and 'hǎo' is the verb meaning 'good.' 'Nǐ hǎo' is an affirmative statement, meaning 'You good.' To form a question, you simply tag a 'ma?' at the end of 'Nǐ hǎo' to get 'Nǐ hǎo ma?', meaning 'You good?', or equivalently, 'How are you?'

an affirmative statement			ma?
subject	**verb**	**complement**	
She/He (Tā)	is (shì)	a teacher (lǎoshī)	ma?
You (Nǐ)	are (shì)	Chinese (Zhōngguórén)	
subject	**verb**	**object**	
Nǐ (You)	hǎo ('good' as verb)		ma?
Lǎoshī (Teacher)	zài ('in' as verb)		
You (Nǐ)	drink (hē)	coffee (kāfēi)	
Wáng xiānsheng (Mr. Wang)	zài ('at' as verb)	jiā (home)	

Note that one of the functions for the word 'do' in English is to help forming questions, but it has no counterpart in Chinese. Thus, in the following exercises you can simply drop 'Do' and add a 'ma?' at the end of each sentence to obtain Chinese equivalent.

Exercise		
1) Do you play ball?	3) Do you have money?	5) Do you Google?
2) Do you <u>subscribe to</u> a newspaper?	4) Do you have time?	6) Do you drive?

Answers: 1) Nǐ dǎ qiú **ma**?   2) Nǐ <u>dìng</u> bàozhǐ **ma**?   3) Nǐ yǒu qián **ma**?   4) Nǐ yǒu shíjiān **ma**?   5) Nǐ Google **ma**?   6) Nǐ kāichē **ma**?

The following table illustrates some variations of 'ma?' when asking for a favor or permission.

Asking for a favor or permission: hǎo ma? = kéyǐ ma? = hǎo bù hǎo?					
adv.	v.	obj.			the rest
Please	wait	a moment/minute/second			?
Qǐng	děng	yí xià			**hǎo ma? / kéyǐ ma? / hǎo bù hǎo?**
Please	give	me	5	minutes	?
Qǐng	gěi	wǒ	wǔ	fēngzhōng	**hǎo ma? / kéyǐ ma? / hǎo bù hǎo?**

5.1.2 Other popular question tags: *ba, ne*

s.	adv.	neg.	v.	adv.	n.	
Wǒmen			qù (go)		chīfàn (eat meal)	
Nǐmen	xiān (first)		chī (eat) / zǒu (leave)			ba.
	Dàgài / Yéxǔ		shì (is) / huì (will, can)			
	(Probably)	bú (not)	/ kéyǐ (okay), etc.			
Nǐ			xìng (surname)		Chén	ba?
Nǐ			chī (eat)	cuò (wrong)	yào (medicine) le	
Nǐ						ne?
	Wèishénme (Why)					[ne]?

Using a 'ba' is a polite way to make a suggestion or guess. For example:

1)   In 'Wǒmen qù chīfàn ba.', it means that you are making a suggestion of going to eat. A 'ba' makes a sentence softer.

2)   'Nín xìng Chén ba?' is used when you are not sure the person you are talking to has the surname Chén.

3)   'Nǐ chī cuò yào le ba?' suggests that the listener has done something extraordinary, either good or bad. Padding with a 'ba?' makes the comment listener-friendly.

The usages for 'ne' are provided in the following:

1)   A 'ne' is used as a question tag for a 'follow-up' question, such as in 'Nǐ ne?' or 'Wèishénme ne?' or 'Nǐ shuō ne?'. These questions will never appear without earlier conversation clues. Just like in a game of 'ping-pong': the originating question uses 'ma' to 'ping' the listener, and the listener uses 'ne' to 'pong' back a 'follow-up' question. But one cannot use 'ne' to 'ping' in an originating question.

2)   However, exceptions happen. For example, you expect many people have arrived before you do, but there are only few there, so you ask, "Where are the people (rén)?" The Chinese version is, "Rén ne?" In this case, the 'ping' part of the 'ping-pong' was preconceived in your mind, and uttering the 'ne' is the 'pong' part.

3)   The 'ne' may also be used as an exclamation point '!', such as in, "Cái bú shì ne! (It's not!)" This 'ne' is not in a question and has nothing to do with the 'ping-pong' routine.

5.2   Questions led by verb 'to be'

English pattern: Are you a teacher?					
be	**subject**		**article**	**noun (complement)**	
Are	you		a	teacher	?

Chinese question phrase: *shì bú shì*

	subject	**be**	**not**	**be**	**article**	**noun**	
(1)	Nǐ (You)	shì	bú	shì	—	lǎoshī (teacher)	?

The answer to this type of question is either 'shì' or 'bú shì'.

Derivatives:					
	subject	be	not	be	noun	
(2)	Nǐ	shì	—	—	lǎoshī (teacher)	ma?
(3)	Nǐ	—	bú	shì		
	subject	be	noun	not	be	
(4)	Nǐ	shì	lǎoshī	bú	shì	?

These four sentences are similar to their English counterparts: (1) Are you or are you not a teacher?
(2) Are you a teacher?   (3) Are you not a teacher?   (4) Are you a teacher or not?

Exercise					
Are you an engineer?					
		bú		gōngchéngshī (engineer)	?
		—	—		ma?
	—	bú			

		—	—		?

Answer: Nǐ shì bú shì gōngchéngshī?   Nǐ shì gōngchéngshī ma?   Nǐ bú shì gōngchéngshī ma?   Nǐ shì gōngchéngshī bú shì?

Derivative: shì ma? (for verifying)

	statement			shì ma?
You	are	[very]	busy,	aren't you?
Nǐ	—	[hěn]	máng,	**shì ma** ?

Exercise

1) He will go to China, **won't he?**	2) We have a meeting tomorrow, **don't we?**

Answer: 1) Tā yào qù Zhōngguó, **shì ma**?   2) Míngtiān (tomorrow) wǒmen yǒu (have) huìyì (meeting), **shì ma**?

Derivative: shì ma? (for expressing a doubt or surprise)

I saw *a big bear* in the park yesterday. Oh, is that true? Really/Very dangerous.				
Yesterday	I	in the park	saw	*a big bear.*
Zuótiān	wǒ	zài gōngyuán lǐ	kànjiàn le	*yì zhī dà xióng.*
Oh,	is that true?	Really dangerous.		
O,	**shì ma?**	Zhēn/Hěn wéixiǎn.		

The Chinese counterpart for 'there be' (is, are,…) is simply 'yǒu' (exist), instead of 'nàlǐ (there) shì (be).' It is because the word 'there' in 'there be' doesn't carry the meaning of 'nàlǐ'. With that being established, the following examples would be easily understood.

English pattern: Are there monsters?

be	subject	noun	
Are	there	monsters	?
subject	**v.**	**noun**	
—	Yǒu (exist)	yāoguài	ma?

Exercise

1) **Are there** problems?	2) Problems?	3) **Are there** red, blue, and white flowers?

Answer: 1) **Yǒu** wèntí ma?   2) **Yǒu** wèntí ma?   3) **Yǒu** hóng de, lán de, hé (and) bái de huā (flower) ma?

In the following examples, the word 'be' is omitted from the Chinese sentences as explained in Chapter 3.

English pattern: Are you busy?

be	subject	adjective		
Are	you	busy		?

Chinese question phrase: *adj. not adj.*

subject		adjective	not	adjective	
You (Nǐ)		busy (máng)		busy (máng)	
		tired (lèi)		tired (lèi)	
		in a hurry (jí)	bu	in a hurry (jí)	?
Your (Nǐde)	house (fángzi)	big (dà)		big (dà)	
This (Zhège)	car (chēzi)	expensive (guì)		expensive (guì)	

The answer to this type of question is either 'adj.' or 'bu adj.'

Derivatives:

s.	adjective	not	adjective	
You (Nǐ)	busy (máng)	—	—	ma?
	—	bù	busy (máng)	

1) Are you hungry?

		bú		?
		—	—	ma?
	—	bú		

2) Is he handsome or not?

		bù		?
		—	—	ma?
	—	bù		

Answer: 1) Nǐ è bú è?   2) Tā yīngjùn bù yīngjùn?

English pattern: Is Chinese difficult to learn?

be	subject	adjective	to + v.	
Is	Chinese	difficult	to learn	?

Chinese question phrase: *adj. not adj.   +   v.*

subject		adj	not	adj.	v.	
Zhōngwén (Chinese)		difficult (nán)	bù	difficult (nán)	learn (xüé)	
This (Zhège) (ge: unit for things)	thing (dōngxī)	good (kěyǐ)	bù	good (kěyǐ)	eat (chī)	?
		pleasant (hǎo)		pleasant (hǎo)		
This (Zhège)	movie (diànyǐng)	pleasant (hǎo)	bù	pleasant (hǎo)	see (kàn)	?
My (Wǒde)	dress (yīfú)				look (kàn)	
Your (Nǐde)	coffee (kāfēi)				drink (hē)	
This (Zhèzhī)	pen (bǐ)				write (xiě)	
Your (Nǐde)	car (chēzi)				drive (kāi)	

| Bowling (Bǎolíng) | ball (qiú) | | | | play (wán) | |

(a) The answer to this type of question is either 'adj. v.' or 'bù adj. v.' (b) **hǎo bù hǎo** can be used in any situation where you ask for an <u>opinion</u> as shown in the above examples. (c) **hǎo bù hǎo** can also be used for asking a <u>favor</u> or <u>permission</u> when placed at the end of a sentence.

Derivatives:

| This (Zhège) movie (diànyǐng) | hǎo | — | — | watch (kàn) | ma? |
| | — | bù | hǎo | watch (kàn) | |

| 1) Is your computer difficult to <u>use</u>? | 2) Is your car fun to <u>drive</u>? | 3) Is Chinese pleasant to <u>learn</u>? |
| | | |

Answer: 1) Nǐde diànnǎo **hǎo bù hǎo** <u>yòng</u>?   2) Nǐde chē **hǎo bù hǎo** <u>kāi</u>?   3) Zhōngwén **hǎo bù hǎo** <u>xüé</u>?

When the adjective has more than one Syllable

subject	adj.	not	adj.	the rest	
This (Zhè) duǒ (unit) flower (huā)	beautiful (měilì)	bù	beautiful (měilì)		?
	měi				
Your (Nǐde) dog (gǒu)	easy (róngyì)		easy (róngyì)	train (xùnliàn)	
	róng				

The answer to this type of question is either 'adj.' or 'bu adj.'.

Derivatives:

subject	adj.	not	adj.	the rest	
This (Zhè) unit (duǒ) flower (huā)	beautiful (měilì)	—	—		ma?
	—	bù	beautiful (měilì)		
Your (Nǐde) dog (gǒu)	easy (róngyì)	—	—	train (xùnliàn)	
	—	bù	easy (róngyì)		

| 1) Are you **glad** that <u>your design</u> *does not have* a problem? | 2) Is it **easy** to assemble a model plane? |
| | |

Answer: 1) Nǐ **gāo bù gāoxìng** <u>nǐde shèjì</u> *méi yǒu* wèntí?   2) Móxíng fēijī **róng bù róngyì** zǔzhuāng?

5.3 Questions led by 'Auxiliary Verb'

In English, an 'auxiliary verb' helps the 'main verb' to ask questions, form negations, and create tenses and voices. Among many auxiliary verbs, we will take the most frequently used ones to demonstrate how they are correlated with Chinese question structures. These are: do, can, may, will, shall, and have. Remember that there is no counterpart in Chinese for auxiliary verb 'do.'

5.3.1 Led by 'Do'

English pattern: Do you watch TV?					
auxiliary verb	**subject**	**main verb**		**noun**	
Do	you	watch		TV	?
Chinese question phrase:		*verb not verb*			
	subject	**verb**	**not**	**verb**	**noun**	
—	You (Nǐ)	watch (kàn)	bu	watch (kàn)	TV (diànshì)	?
		drink (hē)		drink (hē)	coffee (kāfēi)	
		eat (chī)		eat (chī)	sushi (shēngyúpiàn)	
The shortest answer to this type of question is either 'v.' or 'bu v.'						

Derivatives:					
	s.	**verb**	**not**	**verb**	**n.**	
—	You (Nǐ)	watch (kàn)	—	—	movie (diànyǐng)	ma?
		—	bú	watch (kàn)		

Exercise					
1) Do you *play* basketball?					
—			bù		?
2) Do you *want* to go to China?			4) Do you *smoke* cigarettes?		
3) Do you *have* child?			5) Do you *have* a meeting?		

Answer: 1) Nǐ *dǎ bù dǎ* lánqiú.   2) Nǐ *yào bú yào* qù Zhōngguó.   3) Nǐ *yǒu méi yǒu* háizi?   4) Nǐ *xī bù xī* yān?   5) Nǐ *yǒu méi yǒu* huìyì?

Very often in Chinese, more than one verb exists in succession. One reason for this is that Chinese does not have the infinitive form 'to + verb,' thus an infinitive 'to watch' in English becomes just 'watch' in Chinese. As a result, 'want to watch' in English becomes 'want watch' in Chinese. The Chinese question phrase in this case is 'verb₁ not verb₁.'

English pattern: Do you want to eat lunch?					
aux.	**s.**	**verb $_1$**	**verb $_2$**	**object**	
Do	you	want	to eat	lunch	?
Chinese question phrase:		*verb$_1$ not verb$_1$*			
	s.	**verb $_1$**	**not**	**verb $_1$**	**verb $_2$**	**object**	
—	You (Nǐ)	want (xiǎng)	bù	want (xiǎng)	eat (chī)	lunch (wǔfàn)	?

Exercise
We <u>would like</u> to go shopping. Do you **want** to go?

       Answer: Wǒmen <u>xiǎng</u> qù mǎidōngxi. Nǐ **xiǎng bù xiǎng** qù?

When a verb has more than one Syllable

English pattern: Do you Google/Yahoo?

aux.	subject	verb		
Do	you	Google/Yahoo		?

Chinese question phrase: *verb not verb*

	subject	verb	not	verb	the rest	
—	Nǐ (You)	Google/Yahoo Goo /Ya	bu	Google/Yahoo		?
		yùndòng (exercise) yùn		yùndòng		
		zhīdào (know) zhī		zhīdào	I (wǒ) can (huì) fly (kāi) airplane (fēijī)	
		xǐhuān (like) xǐ		xǐhuān	shàng (go to) Zhōngwén (Chinese) kè (class)	
		àichī (love to eat) ài		àichī	hot (là de) stuff (dōngxi)	

Derivatives:

	subject	verb	not	verb	the rest	
—	Nǐ (You)	Google/Yahoo	—	—		ma?
		—	bù	Google/Yahoo		

Exercise

Do you swim?	
1)	2)

      Answer: 1) Nǐ yóuyǒng bù yóuyǒng?   2) Nǐ yóu bù yóuyǒng?

------------------------------ **Culture-Specific Note** ------------------------------

English pattern: Don't you have a meeting?

aux.	s.		v.	object	
Don't	you		have	a meeting	?
Don't	you		recognize	me	?

Chinese question phrase: *bú shì … ma?*

	s.	**bú shì**	v.	object	**ma?**
—	Nǐ	bú shì	yǒu (have)	huìyì (meeting)	ma?
—	Nǐ		rènde (recognize)	wǒ (me)	

Exercise			
1) Don't you have a class?			
	bú shì		**ma?**
2) Don't you want to go to China?			
	bú shì		**ma?**
3) Didn't you say 'whatever'?			
	bú shì		**ma?**

Answer: 1) Nǐ **bú shì** yǒu (have) kè (class) **ma**?   2) Nǐ **bú shì** yào qù Zhōngguó **ma**?   3) Nǐ **bú shì** shuō 'suíbiàn' **ma**?

------------------------------------ End of Note ------------------------------------

5.3.2 Led by the auxiliary verbs other than 'Do'

In this case, the question phrase is 'auxiliary not auxiliary.'

English pattern: May I come in?			
aux.	**subject**	**v.**	
May / Can	I	come in	?

Chinese question phrase: *aux. not aux.*					
subject	**aux.**	**not**	**aux.**	**v.**	
I (Wǒ)	may/can (néng)	bù	néng	jìn lái	?
The shortest answer to this type of question is either 'aux.' or 'bu aux.'					

Derivatives:					
subject	**aux.**	**not**	**aux.**	**v.**	
I (Wǒ)	may/can (néng)	—	—	jìn lái	ma?
	—	bù	néng		

Exercise		
1) **May/Can** I borrow your pen?	2) **Will** you come?	3) **Shall** we go eat?

Answer: 1) Wǒ **néng bù néng** jiè nǐde bǐ?   2) Nǐ **huì (will) bú huì** lái?   3) Wǒmen **yào (shall) bú yào** qù chīfàn (eat)?

In English, when 'have/has/had' are used as **auxiliary verbs**, they help to form the 'perfect tense'. In Chinese, as seen in the following examples, the question phrase **yǒu méi yǒu** works with the perfect tense tag **guò** to form a perfect tense **question**. Refer to Chapter 6 for details on 'Tenses'.

'Have/Has/Had' works as the 'Auxiliary Verb'						
English pattern:		**Has he come yet?**				
aux.	**subject**		**v.**	**obj.**	**the rest**	
Has	he		come			
Have	you		eaten	sushi	[yet]	?
Has	he		been to	China		
Chinese question phrase:		*yǒu méi yǒu ... guò ...*				
subject	**aux.** **yǒu**	**not** **méi**	**aux.** **yǒu**	**v.**	**tag.**	**obj.**
Tā				lái	guò	
Nǐ	yǒu	méi	yǒu	chī	guò	sushi	?
Tā				qù	guò	Zhōngguó	

Derivatives:						
Tā	yǒu	—	—	lái	guò	ma?
Tā	—	méi	yǒu	lái	guò	ma?
Tā	—	—	—	lái	guò	le ma? / méiyǒu?

Besides its role as an auxiliary verb, 'have' also works as a 'main verb' carrying the meaning 'to own'. Its application is exactly the same as the other main verbs. It is interesting that the Chinese for the main verb 'have' is 'yǒu', then by applying the 'v. bu v.' rule for constructing a question sentence, we also get **yǒu méi yǒu**. It is a coincidence that the Chinese 'yǒu' (有) is used for the word 'have' in both 'main' and 'auxiliary' verb usages in English.

'Have' works as the 'Main Verb'					
English pattern:		**Do you have money?**			
aux.	**subject**	**verb**		**object**	
Do	you	have		money	?
Chinese question phrase:		*yǒu méi yǒu*			
	subject	**have**	**not**	**have**	**object**	
—	Nǐ	yǒu	méi	yǒu	qián	?
The shortest answer to this type of question is either 'yǒu' or 'méi yǒu'.						

Derivatives:						
	subject	**have**	**not**	**have**	**object**	
—	Nǐ	yǒu	—	—	qián	ma?
		—	méi	yǒu		

5.4 Questions led by *who, which, what* (Interrogative Pronouns)

Remember that in Chinese the subject always leads the sentence, even in question sentences. Interrogative Pronouns can be used as either subjects or subject complements. For example, in the sentence 'Who wants to go?', 'Who' is the subject, 'wants' is the verb, and 'to go' is the object. This falls into the basic structure of direct correlation.

interrogative pronoun (s.)	verb	obj.	
Who	wants	to go	?
Shéi	yào	qù	

In the case of 'Who is your teacher?', 'your teacher' is the subject and 'Who' is the subject complement. Therefore, in Chinese, the subject 'your teacher' must go to the front of the sentence, and 'Who' goes to the end, for it is a subject complement. This is a cross correlation relationship.

inter. pronoun	v. 'to be'	subject (n.)	
Who	is	your teacher	?
subject		subject complement	
Nǐde lǎoshī	shì	shéi	?

1) **Who** <u>tripped</u> me?	2) **Who** are you?

Answer: 1) **Shéi** <u>bàndǎo le</u> wǒ. 2) Nǐ shì **shéi**.

inter. pronoun	v. 'to be'	subject (n.)	
Which	is	your book	?
subject		subject complement	
Nǐde shū	shì	**nǎ** (which) **yì** (one) **běn** (unit)	?

inter. pronoun (subject)	v. 'to be'	adj. phrase (chap. 3)	
Which	is	no good	?
subject		verb	
Nǎ yí ge	—	bù hǎo	?

1) **Which** is your pencil?	2) **Which** is correct?

Answer: 1) Nǐde qiānbǐ shì **nǎ yì zhī**? 2) **Nǎ yí ge** duì?

inter. pronoun	v. 'to be'	subject (n.)	
What	is	your name	?
subject		subject complement	
Nide míngzi	shì / jiào (call)	shénme	?

1) **What** is this?	2) **What** is your <u>favorite</u> *food*?

Answer: 1) Zhè shì **shénme**?   2) Nǐ[de] <u>zuì xǐhuān de</u> *shíwù* shì **shénme**?

In English, the interrogative pronoun 'what' in the next example functions as the object for the verb 'buy.' Its Chinese counterpart follows the basic 'subject + verb(s) + object' structure. It is a typical example for 'Broken English is perfect Chinese.'

inter. pronoun	aux.	subject	v₁	v₂	object	
What	~~do~~	~~you~~	want	to buy		?
	—	Nǐ	xiǎng	mǎi	**shénme (what)**	?
		You	want	to buy	what	?

1) **What** do you <u>plan</u> to do?	2) **What** do you <u>like</u> to eat?

Answer: 1) Nǐ <u>jìhuà</u> zuò **shénme**?   2) Nǐ <u>xǐhuān/xiǎng</u> chī **shénme**?

------------------------------- **Culture-Specific Note** -------------------------------

English	Chinese
What's the matter?	Zěnme le?
What is it?	
What's wrong? (Shénme cuò le?)	
What happened?	
What's going on?	
What's happening? (greeting)	Zěnmeyàng?
What's up? (greeting)	
What do you want! (hostile)	Nǐ yào zěnmeyàng!
What is this?	Zhè shì shénme?

------------------------------- End of Note -------------------------------

5.5   Questions led by *which, what, whose* (Interrogative Adjectives)

inter. adjective	n.	v. 'to be'	subject (n.)		
Which	book	is	yours		
subject			inter. adjective	n.	?
Nǐde		shì	**nǎ** (which) **yì** (one) **běn** (unit)	shū (book)	

Which pencil is yours?

Answer: Nǐde shì **nǎ yì zhī** (which one unit) qiānbǐ?

inter. adjective	n.	linking v.	subject (n.)	
What	color	is	your car	?
subject		inter. adjective	n.	
Nǐde chēzi	shì	shénme	yánsè (color) [de]	

What is your name? (Culture-Specific)				
subject	v.	inter. adjective	n.	
Nǐ	jiào (are called)	shénme	míngzi (name)	?

What *cuisine* do you <u>want</u> to eat?

Answer: Nǐ <u>xiǎng</u> chī **shénme** *cān*?

inter. adjective	n.	verb 'to be'	subject (n.)	
Whose	stuff	is	this	?
subject		inter. adjective	n.	
Zhè	shì	shéide	dōngxi	?

inter. adjective	n.		
subject		verb	
Whose	stuff	disappeared	?
Shéide	dōngxi	bújiàn le	

Whose hat is this?	

Answer: Zhè shì **shéide** màozi?

5.6 Questions led by *where, when, why, how, how many/much* (Interrogative Adverbs)

To form the Chinese counterpart of the English word 'where,' add a preposition to it, such as 'at where' or 'from where', as illustrated in the following.

s.	inter. adv.		aux.	s.	v.	prep.	
	Where		do	you	go to school	an implied 'at' in Chinese	?
					go to work		
					come	from	
Nǐ	zài (at)	nǎr (where)	—		shàng xüé (go to school)		?
					shàng bān (go to work)		
	cóng (from)	nǎr (where)	—		lái (come)		

s.	inter. adv.	aux. v.	s.	v.	obj.	
	Where	can	I	find	tools	?
Wǒ	**zài** (at) **nǎr** (where)	néng		zhǎodào	gōngjù	

inter. adv.		verb 'to be'	subject (n.)	
Where		is	the library	?
s.			**subject complement**	
Túshūguǎn		[shì]	**zài** (at) **nǎr** (where)	

1) **Where** did you put my keys?	2) **Where** is the restroom?	3) **What (Where)** is the difference?

Answer: 1) Nǐ **zài nǎr** fàng le wǒde yàoshi?   2) Wèishēngjiān [shì] **zài nǎr**? 3) Chābié [shì] **zài nǎr**?   Note: The response to the 'where' question is simply to replace '**nǎr**' with your answer and copy the rest of the question sentence and end with a period as punctuation.

------------------------- **Culture-Specific Note** ----------------------

Where are you going/heading?				
s.	**v.**	**obj.**	**preposition**	
Nǐ	qù (go)	nǎr (where)	—	?
	shàng (go)		qù (to)	
Where were you?				
Nǐ	qù (go)	nǎr (where)	—	le?
	shàng (go)		qù (to)	

------------------------------------ End of Note ----------------------------------

s.	inter. adv.	aux.	s.	v.	obj.	
	When	do	you	start	your new job	?
				go to	China	
Nǐ	**shénme shíhòu**	—		kāishǐ	nǐde xīn gōngzuò	
	(what time)			qù (go to)	Zhōngguó	

1) **When** is the meeting?	2) **When** did you eat lunch?

Answer: 1) Huìyì shì **shénme shíhòu**?   2) Nǐ **shénme shíhòu** chī le wǔfàn?

s.	inter. adv.	aux.	neg.	s.	v.	obj.	
	Why	do	not	you	drink	coffee	?
Nǐ	**wèi (for) shénme (what)**	—	bù		hē	kāfēi	

Why	s.						
Wèi (for) shénme (what)	nǐ	—	bù		hē	kāfēi	

Exercise

1) **Why** *didn't* he come home?	2) **Why** do you *like* country music?

Answer: 1) Tā **wèishénme** *méi yǒu* huí jiā?   2) Nǐ **wèishénme** *xǐhuān* xiāngcūn yīnyüè?

s.	inter. adv.	v. to be	s.	adj.	
	Why	is	he	late	?
Tā	**wèishénme**	—		chídào	

Exercise

1) **Why** is he angry?	
2) **Why** are you *angry* with me?	
3) **Why** is that?	

Answer: 1) Tā **wèishénme** shēngqì?   2) Nǐ **wèishénme** gēn wǒ *shēngqì*?   3) Nà shì **wèishénme** [ne]?

s.	inter. adv.	aux.	s.	v.	n.	
	How	do	I	get/go to	the park	?
			I	exchange	money	
			you	know	him	
Wǒ				qù	gōngyuán	?
Wǒ	**zěnme**	—		huàn	qián	
Nǐ				zhīdào	tā	
	How	can	I	help	you	
Wǒ	**zěnme**	néng		bāng	nǐ	

s.	inter. adv.	aux.	s.	linking v.		
	How	do	you	feel		
				linking v.	complement	?
Nǐ		—		gǎnjüé	zěnmeyàng	

	inter. adv.	v. to be	s.	
	How	is	the food?	
		are	you?	
s.			verb	
Shíwù (Food)		—		
Nǐ		—	zěnmeyàng?	

English pattern: How many apples do you have?					
obj.		aux.	s.	v.	
How many	apples	do	you	have	?
Chinese question word: *jǐ / duōshǎo*					

s.	v.		how many/much	unit	n.	
Nǐ	yǒu (have)		jǐ / duōshǎo	ge	píngguǒ (apple)	?
			duōshǎo	—	qián (money - uncountable noun)	
Nǐ	kàn (watch)	le (past tense tag, see Chap. 6.)	jǐ / duōshǎo	chǎng	diànyǐng (movie)	
	hē (drink)			bēi	kāfēi (coffee)	

Note that 'duō' means 'more' and 'shǎo' means 'less.' In fact, 'duōshǎo' follows the 'true not true' logic to be used in forming a question sentence.

Exercise	
1) **How many** ballgames did you <u>play</u>?	2) **How many** laps did you <u>swim</u>?
3) **How many** letters did you <u>write</u>?	4) **How much** rain did we <u>get</u>?

Answer: 1) Nǐ <u>dǎ</u> le **jǐ/duōshǎo** chǎng (unit) qiúsài?   2) Nǐ <u>yóu</u> le **jǐ/duōshǎo** ge (unit) dānchéng (lap)?   3) Nǐ <u>xiě</u> le **jǐ/duōshǎo** fēng (unit) xìn?   4) Wǒmen <u>dédào</u> le **duōshǎo** yǔ (rain, uncountable)?

-------------------------- **Culture-Specific Note** ---------------------------

'Jǐ,' a common question word, is used to ask for an exact number like the 'x' we use in math problems. No 'ma' is needed at the end of a sentence with 'jǐ' in use. In the following examples, the even number lines are the vocabulary counterparts (not the answers) of the odd number lines.

What time is it [now]?					
s.	verb 'to be'	the rest			
1) [Xiànzài	shì]	**jǐ**	diǎn	[le]	?
2) [Now	is]	x (what)	o'clock (time)	—	
Which week day is today?					
3) Jīngtiān	shì	xīngqī	**jǐ**		?
4) Today	is	weekday	x (what)		
When is your birthday?					
5) Nǐde shēngrì	shì	**jǐ**	yüè	**jǐ**	hào	?
6) Your birthday	is	x (what)	month	x (what)	day	
What is your room number?					
7) Nǐde fángjiān	shì	**jǐ**	hào		?
8) Your room	is	x (what)	number		
What is two plus two?					

9) èr jiā èr	shì	**jǐ**			?
10) 2 + 2	is	x (what)			
How old are your kids?					
11) Nǐde háizimen	[shì]	**jǐ**	suì	[le]	?
12) Your kids	are	x (what)	years old	—	

------------------------------------- End of Note ------------   --------------------

6

The Tenses

English tenses are known for their complexity, but Chinese tenses are relatively simple. The main reason is that Chinese tenses can be spoken and understood by using *explicit* '**time element**,' '**tense indicator**,' and/or '**tense tag**' in a sentence structure, instead of different verb forms. We summarize the English tense types along with their Chinese counterparts in the following to provide a general picture.

English Tense Types		s.	time element	tense indicator	v.	tense tag	the rest	[emphatic tag]
Simple	Present	Wǒ			qù (go to)		yínháng (bank)	
	Present	Wǒ		xiànzài (now)	qù (go to)		yínháng (bank)	
	Past	Wǒ	zuótiān (yesterday)		qù (go to)	le	yínháng (bank)	
	Future	Wǒ	míngtiān (tomorrow)	yào (will)	qù (go to)		yínháng (bank)	
Perfect	Present	Wǒ		[yǐjīng (have already)]	qù (go to)	guò	yínháng (bank)	[le].
	Past	Wǒ	zuótiān (yesterday)	[yǐjīng (had already)]	qù (go to)	guò le	yínháng (bank)	
	Future	Wǒ	míngtiān (tomorrow)	hui (will) [yǐjīng (have already)]	qù (go to)	guò	yínháng (bank)	
Progressive Simple	Present	Wǒ		zài	kàn (read)			
	Past	Wǒ	zuówǎn (last night)	zài	kàn (read)		shū (book)	
	Future	Wǒ	míngtiān (tomorrow)	hui (will) — zài	kàn (read)			
Progressive Perfect	Present	Wǒ		yǐjīng — zài	xiūlǐ (repair)		wǒde fángzi (my house)	
	Past	Wǒ	zuótiān (yesterday)	yǐjīng — zài	xiūlǐ (repair)		yǒu (for) liǎng tiān (two days)	
	Future	Wǒ	míngtiān (tomorrow)	hui yǐjīng — zài	xiūlǐ (repair)			

6.1 Simple Tenses

6.1.1 Simple-Present

s.	v.	the rest of the sentence	English
I (Wǒ)	know (zhīdào)	.	I know.
It (Tiān=Sky)	rains (xiàyǔ)	.	It rains.
He/She (Tā)	goes to (qù)	the bank (yínháng).	He/She goes to the bank.

The emphatic tag 'le'

Although 'le' is a simple little word, it has two important applications. One way is to use it in past tense as the 'past tense tag'.

Another way is to place it at the end of a sentence to emphasize the verb action of the sentence.

s.	v.	the rest of the sentence
Wǒ	zhīdào	le. (to emphasize: I know now.)
Tiān	xiàyǔ	le. (to emphasize: It rains now.)
Tā	qù	yínháng le. (to emphasize: He/She goes to the bank now.)

1) I'm hungry.	4) I like chicken feet.	7) I'm almost finished/done/ready.
2) I'm tired.	5) Too expensive!	8) I'm leaving/going.
3) I'm sick.	6) I'm finished/done/ready.	9) I lost my stuff.

Answer: 1) Wǒ è le. 2) Wǒ lèi le. 3) Wǒ shēngbìng le. 4) Wǒ xǐhuān jī jiǎo le. 5) Tài guì le! 6) Wǒ hǎo le. 7) Wǒ kuài hǎo le. 8) Wǒ qù/zǒu le. 9) Wǒ diū[shī] le wǒde dōngxi le.

'Now' is a simple-present **tense indicator**. In addition to emphatic tag 'le', 'now' gives another layer of emphasis to the verb action of the sentence. The following gives a comparison among them.

s.	tense indicator	v.	the rest	English
Wǒ (I)		dǒng (understand)	.	I understand. (regular)
Wǒ (I)		dǒng (understand)	le.	I understand now. (stronger)
Wǒ (I)	xiànzài (now)	dǒng (understand)	le.	I do understand now. (strongest)

6.1.2 Simple-Past

Past tense tag 'le'

The past tense tag **le** is used to signify that the **verb** happened in the **past**. The rules are:

• Place **le** right after a **verb**.

s.	v.	tag	the rest of the sentence	English
Wǒ	chī (eat)	le	wǔfàn.	I ate lunch.
	zǒu (walk)	le	wǔ (five) lǐ (miles).	I walked five miles.

CHAPTER 6: THE TENSES

qù (go to)	**le**	Zhōngguó.	I went to China.

Le is tagged after the <u>last</u> verb when a sentence has more than one verb.

s.	v₁	v₂	tag	object	English
Tā	qù (go to)	shàng (attend)	**le**	Zhōngwén (Chinese) kè (class).	He went to attend Chinese class.

- The word 'didn't' (méiyǒu) carries past tense information. Therefore, similar to English, the verb after it takes root form, i.e. the **le** is not needed.

s.	neg.	v.	tag	the rest of the sentence	English
Tā	méiyǒu (didn't)	chī (eat)	–	wǔfàn (lunch).	He didn't eat lunch.

Exercise

1) I watched a very good movie.	4) I knew/got it.
2) We finished pronunciation practice.	5) He left.
3) I didn't write this love letter.	6) Didn't you go to class?

Answer: 1) Wǒ kàn **le** yì chǎng (unit) hěn hǎo de diànyǐng. 2) Wǒmen wánchéng **le** fāyīn de liànxí. 3) Wǒ méiyǒu xiě zhè fēng (unit) qíng shū. 4) Wǒ zhīdào **le.** 5) Tā zǒu **le.** 6) Nǐ méiyǒu (didn't) qù shàngkè ma?

- **le** can also be placed at the <u>end</u> of the sentence, depending on the speaker's preference.

s.	v.	the rest of the sentence	tag	English
Tā	qù (go to)	Zhōngguó (China)	**le.**	He went to China.

- The past tense tag (p. t. tag) and emphatic tag (e. tag) may co-exist separately to perform their individual functions.

s.	v.	p. t. tag	the rest	e. tag	English
Tā	chī (eat)	**le**	wǔfàn	**le.**	He ate lunch, indeed.

s.	v.	p. t. tag	the rest	e. tag	English

| Tāmen | guò (cross) | le | hé (river) | le | | They crossed the river. |

- Past tense 'be: was/were' (shì) requires no **le**. Instead, the past tense is presented by a **tense indicator**.

s.	tense indicator	v.	tag	the rest of the sentence		
She		was		a teacher.		
Tā	guòqù (in the past)	shì	–	lǎoshī.		

- There is a culture-specific instance where **le** can be used in non-past tense situations when it is to mean 'completion' of a verb.

s.	time element	v.	tag	the rest of the sentence				
Wǒ	míngtiān	xiě	le	bàogào	zài	qù	nǐ	jiā.
I	tomorrow	write	complete	report,	then	go to	your	house.

Past tense indicator

In addition to the past tense tag **le**, the **time element** and/or **tense indicator** can also be added to further clarify the sentence. The presence of the **time element** is already sufficient. In the following examples, you will see that the **time element** tells us the tense is a **past** one, but the **tense indicator** is added for emphatic effect.

s.	time element	tense indicator	v.	tag	the rest of the sentence
Wǒ					
Wǒ	**zuótiān** (yesterday)		qù (go to)		yínháng (bank).
Wǒ	**zuótiān** (yesterday)	**gānggāng / gāngcái** (just now)		**le**	

6.1.3 Simple-Future

s.	time element	tense indicator	v.	the rest of the sentence
Wǒ	sān nián yǐhòu (three years later)	**jiāng/yaò/huì/ jiāng yaò / jiāng huì** (will)		
		jiānglái yaò/huì (will, in a longer term future)	jiāo (teach)	Zhōngwén (Chinese).

6.2 Perfect Tenses

6.2.1 Present Perfect

Usage 1: To describe a *completed* verb action as of now.

```
-------------|-------------------|-------------------|-------------------> future
       action started     action completed        now
```

Perfect tense tag 'guò'

The word **guò** indicates that the verb is *completed* as of now. It tags immediately after the verb.

	subject	aux. verb 'have'	verb	tag	the rest of the sentence
English:	He	*has*	eat	*en*	lunch.
Chinese:	Tā		chī	**guò**	wǔfàn.

	subject	aux. verb 'have'	verb	tag	the rest of the sentence
English:	I	*have*	see	*n*	that movie.
Chinese:	Wǒ		kàn	**guò**	nàge diànyǐng.

Let's examine a few useful variations:

s.	neg.	verb	tag	the rest of the sentence	English
Tā		chī	guò	wǔfàn **le.**	He has eaten lunch. (**emphatic**)
				wǔfàn le **ma?**	Has he eaten lunch? (**question**)
	méiyǒu (not)			wǔfàn.	He has not eaten lunch. (**negation**)
	méiyǒu (not)			wǔfàn **ma?**	Has he not eaten lunch? (**question**)

1) I have eaten breakfast.

2) I ate breakfast.

3) I have seen that movie *twice.*

4) He hasn't been to the Grand Canyon.

Answer: 1) Wǒ chī **guò** zǎofàn. 2) Wǒ chī le zǎofàn. 3) Wǒ kàn **guò** nàge diànyǐng_liǎngcì. 4) Tā <u>méiyǒu</u> (not) qù (go to) **guò** Dà Xiágǔ.

Perfect tense indicator

A **perfect tense indicator** helps to clarify the tense and also gives an emphatic tone to the sentence. These indicators are words like the following:

1) **yǐjīng** (already): Used in an affirmative sentence for adding emphatic effect and can be optional.

2) **hái** (yet): Used along with '**méiyǒu** (not)' to mean 'not ... yet' in a negation sentence.

s.	tense indicator	neg.	v.	tag	the rest	English
Tā			dú (read)	**guò**	nà (that) běn (unit) shū (book).	He has read that book.
	yǐjīng (already)		dú (read)	**guò**	nà běn shū [**le**].	He has <u>already</u> read that book.
	hái (yet)	**méiyǒu** (not)	dú (read)	**guò**	nà běn shū.	He has <u>not</u> read that book <u>yet</u>.
Wǒ			chī (eat)	**guò**	wǔfàn (lunch).	I have eaten lunch.
	yǐjīng (already)		chī (eat)	**guò**	wǔfàn [**le**].	I have <u>already</u> eaten lunch.
	hái (yet)	**méiyǒu** (not)	chī (eat)	**guò**	wǔfàn.	I have <u>not</u> eaten lunch <u>yet</u>.

3) **céngjīng** (ever) – have ... experience before

4) **bùcéng** (never) – haven't had ... experience before

5) **cónglái méiyǒu** – have never had ... experience before

6) **cónglái bù** – never do ... action

	tense indicator	neg.	v.	tag	the rest	English
Tā	**céngjīng** (ever)		qù (go to)	**guò**	Zhōngguó (China).	He has been to China.
	bùcéng (never)					He has never been to China.
	cónglái	**méiyǒu** (not)				
	cónglái	**méiyǒu** (not)	chī (eat)	**guò**	sushi.	He has never eaten sushi before.
	cónglái	**bù** (not)		–	sushi.	He doesn't eat sushi.

Exercise

1) I have never been to Paris.	2) I used to be an engineer.

Answer: 1) Wǒ cónglái méiyǒu qù guò Bālí.   2) Wǒ céngjīng shì yíge gōngchéngshī.

Usage 2: To indicate that the verb has happened at a past point in time and *continues* to happen now and into the future. In this case, the tag **guò** is not needed, because the verb action is not finished yet. Note, **yǐjīng = have [already]**.

```
-------------------|--------------------------------> future
      happened          now, continues
```

s.	aux.	adv.	v.	prep.	the rest of the sentence	
I	have	[already]	lived	in	New York City	for	many	years.
	tense indicator					
Wǒ	yǐjīng		zhù	zài	Niŭ Yuē Shì	yǒu	xǔduō	nián	[le].

s.	aux.	adv.	v.	prep.	the rest of the sentence	
I	have	[already]	lived	in	New York City	*since 1995.*
		tense indicator				
	time element					
Wǒ	*zìcóng 1995 nián yǐlái*	yǐjīng	zhù	zài	Niŭ Yuē Shì	[le].

1) I have [already] lived in Paris since 2000.	2) I have [already] taken piano lessons *for* five years. (take … lessons = xué)

Answer: 1) Wǒ zìcóng 2000 nián yǐlái yǐjīng zhùzài Bālí [le].   2) Wǒ yǐjīng xué gāngqín yǒu wǔ nián [le].

6.2.2 Past Perfect

Usage: The past perfect tense describes that 'event 1' was *completed* at a past point in time at or before another past reference point - event 2.

```
--------------|----------------------------|--------------------------------> future
    event 1              event 2 (ref. point)                now
```

When	we arrived, (event 2)	the wedding (event 1)	had [already]	started.
Dāng wǒmen (we) dàodá **le** (arrived) *de shíhòu,*		hūnlǐ	**yǐjīng**	kāishǐ le.

Rules: First identify the **time element**, then make the proper choice for a **perfect tense indicator** and add the tag **guò**. The **tense indicator** is for emphatic effect and thus can be optional. Again, the optional [le] at the end of each sentence is the emphatic tag.

s.	time element	tense indicator	v.	tag	the rest	
He			had visited		the Grand Canyon	*many years ago.*
Tā	*xǔduō nián yǐqián*	céngjīng (ever)	yóulǎn	**guò**	Dà Xiágǔ [le].	
He			had visited		the Grand Canyon	*in the past.*
Tā	*guòqù / cóngqián*	céngjīng (ever)	yóulǎn		Dà Xiágǔ [le].	
He			had visited		the Grand Canyon	*in / during 2000.*
Tā	*zài 2000 nián de shíhòu*	céngjīng (ever)	yóulǎn	**guò**	Dà Xiágǔ [le].	
I			had taught		Chinese	*before.*
Wǒ	*Guòqù / cóngqián*	céngjīng (ever)	jiāo (teach)	**guò**	Zhōngwén [le].	
I			had taken (eaten)		my medicine	*this morning.*
Wǒ	*jīntiān zǎoshàng*	yǐjīng (have [already])	chī (eat)	**guò**	wǒde yào [le].	

Exercise

1) I had learned violin before.	2) I had taught Chinese when I was in States.

Answer: 1) Wǒ guòqù céngjīng xúé guò xiǎotíqín.   2) Dāng wǒ zài Měiguó *de shíhòu,* wǒ céngjīng jiāo guò Zhōngwén.

6.3 Progressive (ongoing) Tenses

6.3.1 Progressive Present

s.	tense indicator	v.	the rest of the sentence	English
Wǒ		tīng (listen).		I'm listening.
Wǒ	**zài / zhèngzài**	jiāo (teach)	Zhōngwén (Chinese).	I'm teaching Chinese.
Nǐ		chī (eat)	shénme (what)?	What are you eating?

CHAPTER 6: THE TENSES

1) I am watching TV.	2) I am working.	3) It is raining.	4) What are you reading?

Answer: 1) Wǒ **zài** kàn diànshì.   2) Wǒ **zài** gōngzuò.   3) Tiān (Sky=It) **zài** xiàyǔ (rain).   4) Nǐ **zài** dú shénme?

The verb phrases such as 'be going to' and 'be about to' have different meaning than the pure progressive present tense, and its **tense indicator** is 'zhèngyào.'

1) I am going to go to China.	2) I am about to cancel the meeting.	3) Where are you going?

Answer: 1) Wǒ zhèngyào qù Zhōngguó.   2) Wǒ zhèngyào qǔxiāo nàge huìyì.   3) Nǐ zhèngyào qù nǎr?

An additive **zhe** is used with 'zhèng,' 'zài,' or 'zhèngzài' to emphasize the progressiveness (ongoing motion) of the verb. Note that **zhèng** is an additional word that also works with **zhe**. Again, the tense indicator can be dropped to keep the same meaning but without emphasis.

s.	tense indicator	v.	additive	obj.
Tiān (Sky)	zhèng / zài / zhèngzài	xià (down)	zhe	yǔ (rain).
Wǒ		jiāo (teach)		Zhōngwén (Chinese).
Wǒ		zuò (sit)		kàn diànshì (watch TV).
Nǐ		chī (eat)		shénme (what)?

1) The (that) dog is eating his food.	3) The (that) dog is eating his food in the kitchen.
2) The (that) dog eating his food is mine.	4) The (that) dog is lying in my bed.

Answer: 1) Nàzhī gǒu **zhèng** chī **zhe** tāde shíwù.   2) **Zhèng** chī **zhe** tāde shíwù de nàzhī gǒu shì wǒde.   3) Nàzhī gǒu **zhèng** zài chúfáng lǐ chī **zhe** tāde shíwù.   4) Nàzhī gǒu **zhèng** zài wǒde chuáng shàng tǎng **zhe**.

6.3.2 Progressive Past

s.	time element	tense indicator	v.	the rest	English
Wǒ	qù nián (last year)	zài / zhèngzài	jiāo (teach)	Zhōngwén (Chinese).	I was teaching Chinese last year.
	zuótiān (yesterday)		xiě (write)	xìn (letter).	I was writing a letter yesterday.
	zuó wǎn (last night)		kàn (watch)	diànshì (TV).	I was watching TV last night.

You will see that the time element tells us the progressive tense is a **past** one.

Exercise

1) I was watching a *football game* last night.

2) *What* were you doing yesterday?

3) I was listening to music this morning.

4) *Where* did you live last year?

Answer: 1) Wǒ zuówǎn **zài** kàn *zúqiú bǐsài.* 2) Nǐ zuótiān **zài** zuò *shénme?* 3) Wǒ jīntiān zǎoshàng **zài** tīng yīnyüè. 4) Nǐ qùnián zhù zài *nǎr?* Note: This example is to caution you that 'zài' is the preposition for the verb 'zhù.'

6.3.3 Progressive Future

	time element	tense indicator	v.		time element
I		will	be traveling		all	next month.
Wǒ	xià ge yüè (next month)	huì	dōu (all)	zài lǚxíng (travel).	

Exercise

I'll <u>be writing</u> my thesis *next week.*

Answer: Wǒ *xiàge xīngqī* huì (will) zài xiě (write) wǒde lùnwén.

6.3.4 Progressive Present Perfect

s.	tense indicator	v.	the rest of the sentence

I	have	been fixing		my house	for	two weeks.
Wǒ	yǐjīng	zài	xiūlǐ	wǒde fángzi	yǒu	liǎng ge xīngqī le.

Exercise

I have been planning my wedding *for* over a year.

Answer: Wǒ yǐjīng zài jìhuà wǒde hūnlǐ *yǒu* yì nián duō le.

6.3.5 Progressive Past Perfect

s.	time element	tense indicator	v.		the rest of the sentence			
I		had	been fixing		the roof	for	two hours	before it poured.
Wǒ	zài xià [le] dàyǔ yǐqián	yǐjīng	zài	xiūlǐ	wūdǐng	yǒu	liǎng xiǎoshí le	

Exercise

I *had been studying* Chinese **before** I went to China.

Answer: **Zài** wǒ qù le Zhōngguó **yǐqián**, wǒ *yǐjīng zài xuéxí* Zhōngwén le.

6.3.6 Progressive Future Perfect

I	shall	have	been studying	Chinese	for	two years	by next month.

s.	time element	tense indicator	v.		the rest of the sentence		
Wǒ	dào xià ge yuè wéizhǐ	jiāng	yǐjīng	zài	xuéxí	Zhōngwén	yǒu	liǎng nián le.

Exercise

By next year, I shall *have been doing* this project *for* five years.

Answer: **Dào** míngnián **wéizhǐ**, wǒ jiāng *yǐjīng zài zuò* zhège xiàngmu *yǒu* wǔ nián le.

6.4 Culture-Specific Notes

Present perfect tense for multi-syllable words

A multi-syllable Chinese word can be split into this structure: verb + object (noun). This multi-syllable word format is quite similar to the English usages: walk (v.) the walk (n.) and talk (v.) the talk (n.). The perfect tense expression is shown in the examples. Note that the emphatic tag **le** is dropped when the negation perfect tense indicator 'hái méiyǒu' is used.

		multi-syllable word (used as verb or noun)				
		kǎo|shì (take test)				
		xǐ|zǎo (take bath/shower)				
		chī|fàn (eat meal)				
		kàn|yīshēng (see doctor)				
		dǎ|diànhuà (make phone call)				
		mǎi|cài (buy grocery)				
		shàng|kè (attend class)				
		…etc				
s.	**perfect tense indicator**	**verb**	**tag**	**object**	**tag**	**English**
		kǎo (test)		shì (test)		taken the test.
	yǐjīng (already)	xǐ (wash)		zǎo (bath/shower)		taken a bath.
		chī (eat)		fàn (meal)		eaten a meal.
Wǒ		kàn (see)	**guò**	yīshēng (doctor)	**le.**	seen a doctor.
	hái méiyǒu (not yet) (**le** must dropped)	dǎ (make)		diànhuà (telephone)	(emphatic)	called.
		mǎi (buy)		cài (grocery)		bought grocery.
		shàng (attend)		kè (class)		attended the class.

I have   already   not yet

7

The Conjunctions

A conjunction is a word or a pair of words that connects individual words, phrases, or clauses. The following are examples in English: and, but, or, nor, for, so, yet, after, although, as, because, before, how, if, once, since, than, that, though, till, until, when, where, whether; while some others are in pairs such as, both ... and, either ... or, neither ... nor, not only ... but also, so ... as, and whether ... or.

We study their Chinese counterparts in this chapter.

after = le + [obj.] + yǐhòu,

conj.	clause 1				yǐhòu,	clause 2		
	s.	v.	le	obj.		v.	obj.	the rest of the sentence
	we	eat		dinner,		let's	go	shopping.
After	Wǒmen	chī	le	wǎnfàn	yǐhòu,	wǒmen	qù	guàngjiē ba. (a suggestion tone)

Although 'eat' is in the present tense in English, the word 'after' implies finishing a past event. Thus, in Chinese, a past tense tag **le** is appended to the first verb 'chī' to form 'chī **le**' and to mean 'ate'.

Exercise

1) **After** you finish the homework, you may watch TV.   2) **After** I graduated *from college (university)*, I started to work *for the government*.

Answer: 1) Nǐ zuòwán **le** gōngkè **yǐhòu**, nǐ *cái* (condition tag, an adverb) kěyǐ kàn diànshì.   2) Wǒ *cóng dàxué* bìyè **le yǐhòu**, [wǒ] kāishǐ [le] *wèi zhèngfǔ* gōngzuò.

although = suīrán ..., dànshì ...   synonyms: dànshì = kěshì = búguò

conj.	clause 1		conj.	clause 2		
					still	
Although	it	is raining,	~~but~~	we		go.
Suīrán	tiān (sky)	zài xiàyǔ,	**dànshì**	wǒmen	réngrán	qù.

Exercise

1) **Although** he isn't here, *let's* (go ahead and) start the meeting.   2) **Although** this house is expensive, we still want to buy it.

Answer: 1) **Suīrán** tā bú zài zhèlǐ, **dànshì** *wǒmen* kāishǐ huìyì *ba*.   2) **Suīrán** zhège fángzi [hěn] guì, **dànshì** wǒmen réngrán yào mǎi [tā].

A and B = A hé B   synonyms: hé = gēn = hàn

s.	v.	obj.		
I	eat	beef	and	pork.

Wǒ	chī	niúròu	hé	zhūròu.

Exercise

1) I want to go to Shànghǎi. | 2) I go **with** you.

Answer: 1) Wǒ yào qù Shànghǎi **hé** Běijīng.   2) Wǒ **hé** nǐ **yìqǐ** qù.

as adj. as ... = hé ... yíyàng adj.   synonyms: hé = gēn = xiàng

s.		v.	as	adj.	as	...		yíyàng	adj.
This		is	as	good	as	new.			
Zhè	pair of shoes suāng xiézi	—	hé			new. xīn de		yíyàng	hǎo (good).
You		are	as	beautiful	as	a movie star.			
Nǐ	—		hé			a diànyǐng míngxīng	movie star.	yíyàng	měilì (beautiful).

as soon as = dāng ... gāng ... [de shíhòu], ... jiù ...   synonyms: gāng = zhèng = yī

conj.	clause 1				[de shíhòu],	clause 2			
Dāng	...	gāng	...	to leave,	[de shíhòu],	...	jiù	...	
As soon as	we		ready			it	[immediately]	started	to rain.
Dāng	wǒmen	gāng	zhǔnbèi	zǒu	[de shíhòu],	tiān	jiù	kāishǐ	xiàyǔ le.
As soon as	the children		arrive	home,		they	[immediately]	go to	watch TV.
Dāng	háizimen	gāng	huí dào	jiā	[de shíhòu],	tāmen	jiù	qù	kàn diànshì.

Exercise

1) **As soon as** we arrived home, it started to rain. | 2) We went to cut the grass as **soon as** we finished dinner.

Answer: 1) **Dāng** wǒmen **gāng** dào le jiā [**de shíhòu**], tiān **jiù** kāishǐ xiàyǔ le.   2) **Dāng** wǒmen **gāng** chīwán le wǎnfàn [**de shíhòu**], wǒmen **jiù** qù gē cǎo le.

because = yīnwéi

	clause 1	conj.	clause 2		
			in the past few days	was	too cold.
I	caught a cold	because	the weather	was	too cold.
Wǒ	gǎnmào le	yīnwéi	zài guòqù (past) jǐ (few) tiān (day) lǐ	—	tài lěng le.

1) I *came home* late because the traffic was heavy.   2) I don't want to go because it's not worth it.

Answer: 1) Wǒ chī *huí jiā* yīnwéi jiāotōng hěn yōngjǐ.   2) Wǒ bù xiǎng qù yīnwéi bù zhídé.

because ..., [so] = yīnwéi ..., suǒyǐ   synonyms: suǒyǐ = yīncì

conj.	clause 1			conj.	clause 2			
		are	too high,	[so]	we	will not	go on vacation	this year.
Because	gas prices	are	too high,	[so]	we	will not	go on vacation	this year.
Yīnwéi	yóu jià	—	tài gāo le,	suǒyǐ	wǒmen	jīnnián	bù huì	qù dùjià le.

1) **Because** I was sick, [so] I didn't go to work.   2) **Because** I need cash, [so] I must (have to) go to the bank.

Answer: 1) **Yīnwéi** wǒ shēngbìng le, **suǒyǐ** wǒ méiyǒu qù shàngbān.   2) **Yīnwéi** wǒ xūyào xiànjīn, **suǒyǐ** wǒ bìxū qù yínháng.

before = zài ... yǐqián   synonyms: yǐqián = zhīqián

conj.	clause 1			conj.	clause 2		
	he	entered	this		I	had already	graduated.
Before	he	entered	this	university,	I	had already	graduated.
Zài	tā	jìn le	zhège	yǐqián,	wǒ	yǐjīng	biyè le.

1) You must wash your hands **before** you eat.   2) **Once upon a time**, there was a beautiful princess.

Answer: 1) **Zài** nǐ chīfàn **yǐqián**, nǐ bìxū xǐ [nǐde] shǒu.   2) **Zài** hěn jiǔ (very long time) **yǐqián**, yǒu yíge měilì de gōngzhǔ.

CHAPTER 7: THE CONJUNCTIONS

both <u>noun A</u> and <u>noun B</u> = <u>A</u> hé <u>B</u> dōu   synonyms: hé = gēn = hàn

conj.	n. A	conj.	n. B	adv.	aux.	v.	obj.
Both	he	and	I		will	go to	Shànghǎi.
	Tā	hé	wǒ	dōu	yào	qù	Shànghǎi.

1) **Both** plan A **and** B are good.   2) **Both** squirrels **and** birds live <u>on</u> *trees*.

Answer: 1) Jìhuà A **hé** B **dōu** hǎo.   2) Sōngshǔ **hé** niǎo **dōu** zhù <u>zài</u> *shù* <u>shàng</u>.

both <u>adj. A</u> and <u>adj. B</u> = *yòu* <u>A</u> yòu <u>B</u>   synonyms: (the first) *yòu* = *jì*

	s.	v.	conj.	adj. A	conj.	adj. B
This	apple	is	both	large	and	delicious.
Zhège	píngguǒ	—	yòu	dà	yòu	hǎochī.

1) This movie is **both** long **and** boring.   2) This project is **both** difficult **and** lacking resources.

Answer: 1) Zhège diànyǐng **yòu** cháng **yòu** dāndiào.   2) Zhège xiàngmu **yòu** kùnnán **yòu** quēshǎo zīyuán.

but / however = dànshì   synonyms: dànshì = kěshì = búguò = ránér

	clause 1			conj.	clause 2			
I	drink		tea,	but	I	don't	drink	coffee.
Wǒ	hē		chá,	dànshì	wǒ	bù	hē	kāfēi.
This	painting	is	very beautiful,	but	the price	is		too expensive.
Zhè fú	huà	—	hěn měilì,	dànshì	jiàqián	—	—	tài guì le.

1) This dress is beautiful, **but** it is too expensive.   2) I want to go to your party, **but** I already have <u>another</u> engagement.

Answer: 1) Zhè jiàn yīfú hěn piàoliang, **dànshì** tài guì le.   2) Wǒ xiǎng qù nǐde qìngzhùhuì, **dànshì** wǒ yǐjīng yǒu qítā de yuēhuì le.

[either] noun A or noun B = A or B = A huò B   synonyms: huò = huòshì = huòzhěshì

conj.	n.	conj.	n.	adv.	v. to be	adj.
Either	A	**or**	B		is	good.
	A	huò	B	dōu (all)	—	hǎo.
Neither	A	**nor**	B		is	good.
	A	huò	B	dōu (all) bù	—	hǎo.

A	conj.	B	v.	the rest	English
Nǐ	huò	tā	qù (go)	Shànghǎi.	**Either** you **or** he goes to Shanghai.

s.	v.	A	conj.	B	English
Nǐ	juédìng (decide)	wǒmen	huò	qù bú qù.	You decide we **either** go **or** no go.

1) **Either** plan A **or** plan B, we must pick one.   2) What do you want to eat, [**either**] fried chicken **or** pizza?

Answer: 1) Jìhuà A **huò** B, wǒmen bìxū xuǎnzé yíge.   2) Nǐ xiǎng chī shénme, zhá jī **huò** bǐsà?

either clause A or clause B = búshì A jiùshì B

conj.	clause A		conj.	clause B	
Either	you	win	**or**	I	win.
Búshì	nǐ	yíng	jiùshì	wǒ	yíng.

1) **Either** you die **or** I live. (Chinese usage)   2) **Either** we stay home and watch TV **or** go out to eat and see a movie.

Answer: 1) **Búshì** nǐ sǐ **jiùshì** wǒ huó.   2) **Búshì** wǒmen dāi zài jiā lǐ kàn diànshì **jiùshì** cū qù chīfàn hé kàn diànyǐng.

CHAPTER 7: THE CONJUNCTIONS

for = because = yīnwéi

	clause 1		conj.			clause 2
I	didn't	go,	for	I	was	sick.
Wǒ	méiyǒu	qù,	yīnwéi	wǒ	—	shēngbìng le.

if = rúguǒ … [de huà]   synonyms: rúguǒ = yàoshi

conj.	clause 1		[conj.]			clause 2		
					would	also	go	with you.
If	you	would	go, [de huà],	I				
Rúguǒ	nǐ	yào	qù [de huà],	wǒ	yě	yào	hé nǐ yīqǐ (together)	qù.

If it weren't for …, = Rúguǒ bú shì yīnwéi … [de huà],   synonyms: rúguǒ = yào

conj.	clause 1		[conj.]			clause 2
If	it weren't	for	you, [de huà],	I	would have	failed.
Rúguǒ	bú shì	yīnwéi	nǐ [de huà],	wǒ	yǐjīng	shībài le.

Exercise

If it weren't for [the fact] that I have cash, we wouldn't be able to return to the hotel.

Answer: **Rúguǒ bú shì yīnwéi** wǒ yǒu xiànjīn [de huà], wǒmen yěxǔ bù néng huí dào bīnguǎn le.

neither verb A … nor verb B … = jìbu verb A … yěbu verb B …

s.	conj.	verb A	obj.	conj.	verb B	obj.
I	neither	go to	Běijīng	nor	go to	Shànghǎi.
Wǒ	jìbu	qù	Běijīng	yěbu	qù	Shànghǎi.
He	neither	smokes		nor	drinks.	
Tā	jìbu	xīyān		yěbu	hējiǔ.	

neither verb A … nor verb B … = méiyǒu verb A … yěméiyǒu verb B … {for past event only}

s.	conj.	verb A	obj.	conj.	verb B	obj.

I		neither	went to	Běijīng	nor	went to	Shànghǎi.
Wǒ		méiyǒu	qù	Běijīng	yěméiyǒu	qù	Shànghǎi.

neither A nor B = jìbúshì A yěbúshì B

conj.	clause A		[conj.]	clause B	
				clause B	
Neither	you	win	**nor**	I	win.
Jìbúshì	nǐ	yíng	**yěbúshì**	wǒ	yíng.

s.	v.	conj.	noun phrase A		conj.	noun phrase B	
It	is	**neither**	your	mistake	**nor**	my	mistake.
		Jìbúshì	nǐde	cuò	**yěbúshì**	wǒde	cuò.

Exercise

1) I **neither** play tennis **nor** hockey.

2) He **neither** went to your house **nor** my house.

3) Our success is *due to* **neither** resources **nor** timing, but team work.

4) **Neither** you **nor** I was wrong.

Answer: 1) Wǒ **jìbù** dǎ wǎngqiú **yěbù** dǎ bīngqiú. 2) Tā **méiyǒu** qù nǐ jiā **yěméiyǒu** qù wǒ jiā. 3) Wǒmen de chénggōng **jìbúshì** *yóuyú* zīyuán **yěbúshì** *yóuyú* shíjī, *érshì* yóuyú tuánduìjīngshén. 4) **Jìbúshì** nǐ **yěbúshì** wǒ cuò le.

nor = yěbù;　　nor = yěméiyǒu { used with 'didn't' only}

	clause 1			clause 2
You	don't	like	sushi,	**nor** do I.
Nǐ	bù	xǐhuān	sushi,	wǒ **yěbù** xǐhuān sushi.

Exercise

1) He doesn't like Jenny, **nor** does Paul.

2) He *didn't* go, **nor** did I.

Answer: 1) Tā bù xǐhuān Jenny, Paul **yěbù** xǐhuān Jenny. 2) Tā *méiyǒu* qù, wǒ **yěméiyǒu** qù.

CHAPTER 7: THE CONJUNCTIONS

not only ... but also ... = bù jǐn ... érqiě [yě] ...   synonyms: bùjǐn = búdàn

s.	v. to be	conj.	adj. phrase	conj.
This stuff	is	**not only**	too expensive,	**but also**
Zhège dōngxi	—	**bù jǐn**	tài guì le,	**érqiě [yě]**

	adj. phrase	
not	easy	to use.
bù	róngyì/hǎo	yòng.

Exercise

1) The product is **not only** easy to use **but also** inexpensive.

2) He **not only** plays guitar **but also** plays piano. (emphatic)

Answer: 1) Zhège chǎnpǐn **bù jǐn** róngyì/hǎo yòng **érqiě [yě]** bú guì.   2) Tā **bù jǐn** huì tán jítā **érqiě [yě]** huì tán gāngqín.

or = háishi (only in questions)   synonyms: háishi = huò = huòshi = huòzhěshì

s.	conj.	s.	aux.	v.	obj.	English
Nǐ	**háishi**	tā	yào (will)	qù (go to)	Shànghǎi?	Will you or him go to Shànghǎi?

s.	v.	conj.	obj.	obj.	English
Nǐ	xǐhuān (like)	**háishi**	Běijīng	Shànghǎi?	Do you like Běijīng or Shànghǎi?
Nǐ	yào (want)	**háishi**	hóngsè (red) de	huángsè (yellow) de?	Do you want red or yellow?

Exercise

1) Do we turn left **or** right?

2) Do you like sour **or** hot?

Answer: 1) Wǒmen zhuǎn zuǒ **háishì** yòu?   2) Nǐ xǐhuān [chī] suān de **háishì** là de?

otherwise = fǒuzé ... [jiù] (emphatic)   synonyms: fǒuzé = yàobùrán

clause 1				conj.	clause 2			
We	must	walk	faster,	**otherwise**	we		will be	late.
Wǒmen	bìxū	zǒu	kuài yìdiǎnr,	**fǒuzé**	wǒmen	**[jiù]**	yào	chí le.

Exercise

1) We must rest *a little*, **otherwise** we *will* be exhausted.

2) Be patient, **otherwise** you *may* worsen the problem.

Answer: 1) Wǒmen bìxū xiūxí *yíxià*, **fǒuzé** wǒmen [**jiù**] *huì* lèihuài le.   2) Yào rěnnài, **fǒuzé** nǐ *kěnéng huì* èhuà wèntí.

since ... then = jìrán ... nàme ... jiù ... le (jiù ... le: emphatic)

conj.	clause 1				conj.	clause 2					
Since	you	decided	not	to go,	**[then]**	we		will not	force	you.	
Jìrán	nǐ	juéding le	bú	qù,	**nàme**	wǒmen	**jiù**	bú yào	miǎnqiǎng	nǐ	**le.**

Exercise

1) **Since** you decided not to go, **then** we are leaving without you.   2) **Since** you don't need this tool, **then** we'll take it *away*.

Answer: 1) **Jìrán** nǐ juéding le bú qù, **nàme** wǒmen **jiù** zuǒ **le.**   2) **Jìrán** nǐ bù xūyào zhège gōngjù, **nàme** wǒmen **jiù** yào *ná zǒu* **le.**

still = háishì   synonym: háishì = réngrán

	clause 1	conj.	clause 2		
It	is raining,	**still**	we	will	go.
Tiān	zài xiàyǔ,		wǒmen	yào	qù.

háishì (used as an adverb in Chinese)

Exercise

1) Although it's late, we **still** continue to play cards.   2) Although it's been very difficult, he **still** presses on unceasingly.

Answer: 1) Jǐnguǎn shíjiān (time) wǎn le, wǒmen **háishì** jìxù wán pái.   2) Jǐnguǎn yǐjīng hěn kùnnán le, tā **háishì** bùtíng dì xiàngqián (forward) zǒu (walk).

then = nàme

clause 1				conj.	clause 2
I	don't	like	to eat	sushi,	**[then]** what about you?
Wǒ	bù	xǐhuān	chī	sushi,	**nàme** nǐ ne?

Exercise

CHAPTER 7: THE CONJUNCTIONS

93

1) If you don't want it, [then] I *will* take it.	2) If you don't go, [then] I don't go either.

Answer: 1) <u>Rúguǒ</u> nǐ bú yào [dehuà], **nàme** wǒ [jiù (emphatic)] *yào* ná le.   2) <u>Rúguǒ</u> nǐ bú qù [dehuà], **nàme** wǒ yě bú qù le.

therefore = suǒyǐ   synonym: suǒyǐ = yīncǐ

clause 1			conj.	clause 2		
			therefore			
I	was	sick,	therefore	I	couldn't/didn't	go to class.
Wǒ	—	shēngbìng le,	**suǒyǐ**	wǒ	bùnéng/méiyǒu	qù shàngkè.

Exercise

1) The company *did very well* <u>this year</u>, **therefore** we all *received* bonuses.
2) It is <u>about to</u> rain, **therefore** we must cancel the baseball game.

Answer: 1) Gōngsī <u>jīnnián</u> *zuò de hěn hǎo*, **suǒyǐ** wǒmen dōu *shōudào le* jiǎngjīn.   2) Tiān <u>jiù yào</u> xiàyǔ le, **suǒyǐ** wǒmen bìxū qǔxiāo bàngqiú bǐsài.

unless = chúfēi   synonyms: only if

clause 1				conj.	clause 2			
You	cannot	play	video games,	**unless**	you	finished	your	homework.
Nǐ	bù néng	wánr	diànshì yóuxì,	**chúfēi**	nǐ	zuòwán le	nǐde	zuòyè.

Exercise

1) We cannot release the product, **unless** we resolved the intermittent problem.
2) We can't go/leave, **unless** we <u>all</u> received our passports.

Answer: 1) wǒmen bù néng fāngxíng chǎnpǐn, **chúfēi** wǒmen jiějué le duànxù de wèntí.   2) Wǒmen bù néng qù/zǒu, **chúfēi** wǒmen dōu shōudào le wǒmen de hùzhào.

until = zhídào clause wéizhǐ

clause 1	conj.	clause 2	conj.

We	will	continue	to test it,	until	we	are able to (can)	obtain	a	reliable	result.	
wǒmen	yào	jìxù	cèshì [tā]	zhídào	wǒmen	néng	dédào	yíge	kěkào de	jiéguǒ	wéizhì.

clause				prep. (L)	object	prep. (R)
We	will	continue	to test it	until	midnight.	
wǒmen	yào	jìxù	cèshì [tā]	zhídào	wǔyiè	wéizhì.

1) Please continue to search for it **until** we find it.

2) Please continue to search for it **until** dusk.

Answer: 1) Qǐng jìxù xúnzhǎo [tā] **zhídào** wǒmen zhǎodào tā **wéizhì**.   2) Qǐng jìxù xúnzhǎo [tā] **zhídào** huánghūn **wéizhì**.

when = dāng ... de shíhòu   synonyms: while, as

conj.	clause 1				clause 2		
When	I	was	little,		I	often	was	sick.
Dāng	wǒ	—	xiǎo	**de shíhòu,**	wǒ	chángcháng	—	shēngbìng.

1) **When** it rains, it <u>pours</u>.

2) Please <u>take off</u> your shoes **when** you *come in*.

Answer: 1) **Dāng** tiān xiàyǔ **de shíhòu**, tiān jiù (emphatic) <u>xià dà yǔ</u>.   2) **Dāng** nǐ *jìn lái* **de shíhòu**, qǐng <u>tuō xià</u> nǐde xiézi.

whether ... or not = shìfǒu

clause 1				conj.	clause 2			conj.
I	am	not	sure	**whether**	the store	is	open	**or not.**
Wǒ	—	bú	quèdìng	**shìfǒu**	shāngdiàn (s.)	—	kāimén (v.).	**shìfǒu**

1) I don't know **whether** he <u>will</u> come **or not**.

2) **Whether** you <u>commit</u> **or not** decides the fate of this project.

Answer: 1) Wǒ bù zhīdào tā **shìfǒu** <u>huì</u> lái.   2) Nǐ **shìfǒu** <u>chéngnuò</u> juédìng zhège xiàngmu de mìngyùn.

(same person) doing **A** while doing **B** = yìmiàn **A** yìmiàn **B**   synonym: yìmiàn = yìbiān

	conj.	doing A	conj.	doing B
We		are eating	while	watching	TV.
Wǒmen	**yìmiàn**	chī wǎnfàn	**yìmiàn**	zài kàn diànshi.

Exercise

1) The kids <u>are surfing the Internet</u> **while** doing homework.   2) He is walking <u>on</u> the treadmill **while** reading a book.

Answer: 1) Háizimen **yìmiàn** <u>zài shàngwǎng</u> **yìmiàn** zài zuò zuòyè.   2) Tā **yìmiàn** <u>zài zǒulùjī shàng</u> zǒu **yìmiàn** zài kàn shū.

8

Culture-Specific
Chinese Words & Phrases

By mastering this chapter, you will be promoted from the level of speaking 'Very Good Chinese' to a new level – speaking 'Chinese Chinese.'

In previous chapters we have been learning Chinese via English through the help of sentence structure correlation between the two languages: direct correlation and cross correlation. In this chapter we will introduce the third characteristic: *culture-specific* Chinese words and phrases that are unique only to the Chinese language. Although the culture-specific Chinese words and phrases do not have their English counterpart, the <u>direct correlation</u> and <u>cross correlation</u> sentence structure relationship still holds with only few exceptions. The following summarizes the most frequently used sentence structures common to both Chinese and English:

CHAPTER 8: CULTURE-SPECIFIC CHINESE WORDS & PHRASES

1. Subject + verb (direct correlation)
2. Subject + verb + object/specifier/complement (direct correlation)
3. Transitive verb + object (direct correlation)
4. Intransitive verb + preposition + object (direct correlation)
5. Auxiliary verb (v_1) + main verb (v_2) + infinitive verb (v_3) (direct correlation)
6. Specifier + specifyee (direct correlation)
7. Specifyee + specifier (cross correlation)

In the following, we examine the culture-specific Chinese words and phrases, and you will see that the sentence structures are much inline with what has been summarized above with only few exceptions. Please note that the English sentences may look awkward because we are dealing with the culture-specific part of the language.

bǎ		synonym: bǎ = jiāng	
s.	**v.**	**obj.**	
I	mopped	the floor.	
Wǒ	cā le	dìbǎn.	
	v_1 (additive)	**obj.**	**v_2**
Wǒ	**bǎ**	dìbǎn	cā le.
s.	**v.**	**obj.**	
That dog	ate	my ice cream!	
Nàzhī gǒu	chī le	wǒde bīng qílín!	
	v_1 (additive)	**obj.**	**v_2**
Nàzhī gǒu	**bǎ**	wǒde bīng qílín	chī le!

1) I *completed* my project.	2) Please *pick up* the trash *on the floor.*

Answer: 1) Wǒ **bǎ** wǒde xiàngmù *wánchéng le.*   2) Qǐng **bǎ** *zài dìbǎn shàng de lājī* jiǎn qǐlái.

bǎ ... [gěi]   synonym: bǎ = jiāng

	v₁	obj.	adv.	v₂	English
Wǒ	bǎ	dìbǎn	[gěi]	cā le (mopped).	I mopped the floor.
Nàzhī gǒu		wǒde bīng qílín		chī le (ate)!	That dog ate my ice cream!
				3) I solved the problem.	
				4) He repaired the car.	

1) I cleaned the table.

2) I cleaned the house.

Answer: 1) Wǒ **bǎ** zhuōzi [**gěi**] cāgānjìng le.   2) Wǒ **bǎ** fángzi [**gěi**] dǎsǎo le.   3) Wǒ **bǎ** wèntí [**gěi**] jiějué le.   4) Tā **bǎ** chēzi [**gěi**] xiūlǐ le.

bèi ... [gěi] ... = by (passive voice)   synonym: bèi = ràng = gěi

s.	aux.	v.	prep.	obj.	the rest of the sentence
I	was	bitten	by	a mosquito	.

	v₁	obj.	adv.	v₂	
Wǒ	**bèi**	wénzi (mosquito)	[**gěi**]	yǎo / dīng (bite)	le.
	gěi		---		

s.	aux.	v.	prep.	obj.	the rest of the sentence
My window	was	broken	by	a neighbor's kid	.

	v₁	obj.	adv.	v₂	
Wǒde chuānghu	**bèi**	línjū de háizi	[**gěi**]	dǎpò (break)	le.
	gěi		---		

1) My car was hit by a deer.

2) He was elected as chairman by the members.

CHAPTER 8: CULTURE-SPECIFIC CHINESE WORDS & PHRASES

Answer: 1) Wǒde chē **bèi** yīzhī lù [**gěi**] zhuàng le.　　2) Tā **bèi** huìyuánmen [**gěi**] xuǎn wéi zhǔxí.

A bǐ B + adj. = A is more adj. than B　　(bǐ = a verb 'than')

Chinese				English				
A (s.)	**bǐ**	**B (obj.)**	**adj.**	**A**	**is**	**adj.-er**	**than**	**B**
Júzi (Orange)	bǐ	níngméng (lemon)	tián (sweet).	Orange	is	sweeter	than	lemon.

Chinese					English				
A (s.)	**bǐ**	**B (obj.)**	**adj.**		**A**	**is**	**adv.**	**adj.-er**	**than**	**B**
Júzi (Orange)	bǐ	níngméng (lemon)	tián (sweet)	de duō (more). / duō le. / de [bu] duō. / yìdiǎnr.	Orange	is	much / [not] much / a bit	sweeter	than	lemon.
Wǒde chē (car)	bǐ	tāde chē	xiǎo (small)	de duō (more). / duō le. / de [bu] duō. / yìdiǎnr.	My car	is	much / [not] much / a bit	smaller	than	his car.

A	bǐ	B	v.		adv.		English
	bǐ		**v.**		**adv.**		
Tā	bǐ	wǒ	pǎo (run)	de	kuài (fast)	duō (more) le.	He runs much faster than I do.

1) He is a bit taller **than** I.　　2) He is a lot shorter **than** I.　　3) He eats much *slower* **than** I do.

Answer: 1) Tā **bǐ** wǒ gāo yìdiǎnr.　　2) Tā **bǐ** wǒ ǎi de duō.　　3) Tā **bǐ** wǒ chī de *màn* duō le.

bǐjiào = more

s.	v. to be	adv.	adj.	English
Zhège píngguǒ (This apple)	~~shì (is)~~	bǐjiào (**more**)	tián (sweet).	This apple is **sweeter.**
Zhè yíge (This one)			**hǎo (good).**	This one is **better.**
Tāde chē (His car)			guì (expensive).	His car is **more** expensive.
Zhège wèntí (This problem)			máfán (troublesome).	This problem is **more** troublesome.

1) This project is more difficult.   2) He eats slower.   3) I am shorter.

Answer: 1) Zhège xiàngmù **bǐjiào** nán.   2) Tā chī de **bǐjiào** màn.   3) Wǒ **bǐjiào** ǎi.

bié = (1) imperative 'don't'; (2) adjective: other

	adv.	v.	obj.	the rest	English
	Bié (Don't)	kāi (crack)	wánxiào (joke)	le!	**Don't** joke! (playfully)
		guài (blame)	tā (him)	le.	**Don't** blame him.

s.	v.	adj.	n.		English
Nǐ	yǒu (have)	**bié** (other) de	yàngzi (style)	ma?	Do you have **other** styles?

1) **Don't go in!**   2) **Don't mess things up!**   3) **Other** people also bought it.

Answer: 1) **Bié** jìn qù!   2) **Bié** luàn lái!   3) **Bié** [de] rén yě mǎi le.

bìng bu = actually don't

s.	adv.	v.	the rest of the sentence	English	
Wǒ	**bìng** (actually)	bu (don't)	xūyào (need)	qù (go to) kāihuì (meeting).	I actually don't — need to go to the meeting.
			jièyì (mind)	.	mind.
			xǐhuān (like)	chī (eat) bīngqílín (ice cream).	like to eat ice cream.
		méiyǒu (didn't)	xiě (write)	xìn (letter).	I actually didn't — write the letter.

bìng bú shì = actually isn't

s.	adv.	v.	the rest of the sentence	English
Tā	**bìng** (actually)	**bú shì** (was not)	hěn (very) gāoxìng (happy).	He actually wasn't very happy.

CHAPTER 8: CULTURE-SPECIFIC CHINESE WORDS & PHRASES

bìng méi yǒu = actually don't have

s.	adv.	v.	the rest of the sentence	English
Tā	bìng (actually)	méi yǒu (doesn't have)	hěnduō (many) péngyǒu (friends).	He actually doesn't have many friends.

bìng méi yǒu = actually didn't (for past event only)

s.	adv.	v.	the rest of the sentence	English
Tā	bìng (actually)	méi yǒu (didn't)	lái (come).	He actually didn't come.

1) I actually don't want to speak.   2) That movie actually wasn't very good.

Answer: 1) Wǒ **bìng bù** xiǎng shuōhuà.   2) Nàge diànyǐng **bìng bú shì** hěn hǎokàn.

cái = only   synonym: cái = zhǐ[yǒu]

s.	v.	adj.	the rest of the sentence	English
Tā	shì (is)	cái (only)	wǔ (five) suì (years old).	He is **only** 5 years old.

A cái B = not B until A

s.	A	cái	B	(He)	not	B	until	A
Tā	[gānggāng (just now)]	cái	dào/lái (arrive/come).	He did	not	arrive/come	until	just now.
	jīntiān wǎnshàng (this evening)		qǐchuáng (get up).		not	get up	until	this evening.
		cái	néng (can) lái (come).	He can	not	come	until	this evening.
	zǒu le (traveled) wǔ tiān (five days)		dào (arrive).	He did	not	arrive	until	traveled for five days.

cái = then (conditional)   synonym: cái = cái huì = cái néng = cái kěyǐ

Rúguǒ (**If**) nǐ guāi (behave),	wǒ **cái (then)** huì (will)	gěi (give) nǐ tángguǒ (candy).	**If** you behave, **then** I *will* give you candy.

1) The game started only two minutes.	3) We didn't start dinner until just now.
2) He will not be able to arrive until another ten minutes.	4) If he succeeded, then we are okay to start.

Answer: 1) Bǐsài kāishǐ le **cái** liǎng fēngzhōng.   2) Tā zài (another) shí fēngzhōng **cái** néng dào.   3) Wǒmén gānggāng **cái** kāishǐ chī wǎnfàn.   4) Rúguǒ tā chénggōng le, wǒmén **cái** kěyǐ kāishǐ.

chī (eat) medicine = take medicine

s.	v.	perfect tense tag	obj.	the rest	English
Ni	chī le		yào (medicine)	ma?	Did you take medicine?
Wǒ	chī	guò	wǒde yào		I have taken my medicine.
		guò le		le.	I had taken my medicine.

cóng … lái = come from …   synonym: cóng = yóu

s.	prep.	obj.	v.	English
Ni	**cóng** (from)	nǎli (where)	**lái** (come)?	*Where do you* **come from**?
Wǒ	**cóng** (from)	Niǔ Yuē (New York)	**lái** (come).	I **come from** *New York*.

cóng … dào … = from … to …

cóng	…	dào	…	the rest of the sentence		meaning
Cóng (from)	zuǒ (left)	**dào**	yòu (right)	dōu (all) shì (are)	hóng (red) de.	**From** left **to** right are all red.
	shàng (top)	**dào** (to)	xià (down)		tānwū (corrupted) de.	**From** top **to** down are all corrupted.
	lǐ (inside)		wài (outside)		xīn de (new).	**From** inside **to** outside are all new.

1) Time is **from** forever **to** forever.	2) How far is it **from** Běijīng **to** Shànghǎi?

Answer: 1) Shíjiān shì **cóng** yǒngyuǎn **dào** yǒngyuǎn.   2) **Cóng** Běijīng **dào** Shànghǎi yǒu duō yuǎn?

CHAPTER 8: CULTURE-SPECIFIC CHINESE WORDS & PHRASES

chúle ... yǐwài = besides = in addition to

Besides	John,		I	also	invited	Mary.
Chúle	Yuēhàn	yǐwài,	wǒ	yě	yāoqǐng le	Mary.

Exercise

Besides Chinese, I also can speak English.

Answer: **Chúle** Zhōngwén **yǐwài**, wǒ yě huì shuō Yīngwén.

dào = verb: arrive

s.	v.			the rest of the sentence	English
Tā	dào			le.	He arrived.
	inter. adverb	v₁	v₂		
Tā	shénme shíhòu (when)	huì (will)	dào (arrive)	?	When will he arrive?

dào = result verb: reach at the target

s.	v₁	v₂	result verb	the rest of the sentence	English		
Wǒ	néng/kěyǐ (can)	tīng (hear)	dào/jiàn	[tā].	I can	hear	
		kàn (see)				see	it.
		wén (smell)				smell	

dào destination qù = go to destination   synonym: dào = shàng = wǎng

s.	v.	destination	prep.	the rest of the sentence	English
Wǒ	dào	yínháng (bank)	qù	.	I **go to** the bank.
Nǐ		nǎlǐ/nǎr		?	Where do you **go to**? = Where are you going?
Wǒ		shūjú		.	I **go to** the bookstore.

s.	v.	destination		the rest of the sentence	English
Nǐ	qù	nǎlǐ/nǎr	—	?	Where do you **go to**? = Where are you going?

Wǒ		yínháng	.	I **go** to the bank.

1) I **go to** supermarket.	2) He **goes to** gym to do exercise.	3) I don't **go to** anywhere.

Answer: 1) Wǒ **dào** chāojí shìchǎng **qù**. 2) Tā **dào** tǐyùguǎn **qù** zuò yùndòng. 3) Wǒ bú **dào** nálǐ **qù**.

dào destination lái = come to destination

s.	time adv.	v₁	v₂	destination	prep.	the rest	English
			dào		lái		
Nǐ	míngtiān (tomorrow)	huì (will)	lái (come to)	bàngōngshì (office)	—	ma?	Boss: Will you **come to** office tomorrow?
Wǒ			dào		qù		You: I will **go to** office tomorrow.
			qù (go to)		—	.	

Exercise

1) I want to **go to** Shànghǎi.	2) Please **come** here.

Answer: 1) Wǒ xiǎng **dào** Shànghǎi **qù**. 2) Qǐng **dào** zhèlǐ **lái**.

dàyuē … zuǒyòu = about/around/or so

s.	v.	adv. phrase			English
		dàyuē		zuǒyòu.	
Zhège dōngxi (stuff)	zhí (worth)	—	wǔ bǎi (500) kuài	zuǒyòu.	This stuff is worth of **about** 500 bucks.
			dàyuē	.	

s.	time adv. phrase			English	v.	obj.
	dàyuē				zuǒyòu	
Wáng jiā (The Wang's family)	—	zài (at) wǎnshàng (evening) qī diǎn (7 o'clock)			zuǒyòu	chī (eat)
	dàyuē				—	wǎnfàn (dinner).

104

CHAPTER 8: CULTURE-SPECIFIC CHINESE WORDS & PHRASES

105

Exercise

1) He will arrive at 10AM or so.	2) I guess she is **about** thirtish.

Answer: 1) Tā yào zài **dàyuē** zǎoshàng shí diǎn **zuǒyòu** dàodá.   2) Wǒ cāi tā **dàyuē** sānshí **zuǒyòu**.

de = an adjective tag

s.	v₁	v₂	number/unit	adj.		the rest		English
Wǒ	xǐhuān (like)	kàn (read)	—	pēngrèn (cook)		shū (book).		I like to read cookbooks.
Wǒmēn	qù (go) le	—	yíge (a)	měilì (beautiful)	**de**	gōngyuán (park).		We went to a beautiful park.
Zhè (This)	shì (is)	—	yìduǒ (unit for flowers) (a)	hóng[sè] (red)		méigui (rose).		This is a red rose.
Wǒde lǎoshī	shì (is)	—	yíge (a)	nǚ	**de**	rén (people).		My teacher is a woman.

de = an adjective tag for Possessive Adjectives: my, his, her, our, their, Mr. Wang's, …

s.	v.	adj.	the rest of the sentence
Wǒ	shì (am)	nǐde (your)	lǎoshī (teacher).
Nǐ	shì (are)	wǒde (my)	xuéshēng (student).

Exercise

1) This is **mine**.	3) I *have not seen* that woman *before.*	5) This is **my** bicycle.
2) This is lǎo Wáng's stuff.	4) I like to read **hunting** books.	6) This is that table's leg.

Answer: 1) Zhè shì **wǒde**.   2) Zhè shì Lǎo Wáng **de** dōngxi.   3) Wǒ yǐqián *méiyǒu jiàn guò* nàge nǚ **de**.   4) Wǒ xǐhuān kàn **dǎliè de** shū.   5) Zhè shì **wǒde** zìxíngchē.   6) Zhè shì nàge zuōzi **de** tuǐ.

'shi ... de' sandwich (also see Culture-Specific Note §3.7.2)

	Shi (is)			Yes.
Bú (not)	shi		de.	No.
			—	

s.	v. to be	v.	obj.	adj.		noun		English
Wǒde lǎobǎn	shi			nǚ	de	rén.		My boss is a woman.
Tā	shi	dǎ (catch)	yú (fish)		de	rén.	de	He's a fisherman.
		yǒu (has)	qián (money)					He's a rich man.
		zuò (do)	gōng (labor work)					He's a blue-collar worker.
		chī (eat)	sù (meatlessness)					He's a vegetarian.
Zhège (This) tāng (soup)	shi	tián (sweet)					de.	This soup is sweet.
Zhè (This)		kěxiào (ridiculous)					de.	This is ridiculous.
Zhè (This)		bùkěnéng (impossible)						This is impossible.

1) I am a programmer.	2) He is a pilot.	3) Grapefruit is bitter sweet.

Answer: 1) Wǒ **shi** yíge xiě ruǎnjiàn **de**. 2) Tā **shi** yíge kāi fēijī **de**. 3) Pútáoyòu **shi** kǔ tián **de**.

s.	shi	...	v.	de	English
Nǐ	shi	cóng (from) nǎr (where)	lái (come)	de?	Where do you come from?
Wǒ	shi	cóng (from) Niǔ Yuē	lái (come)	de.	I come from New York.
Nǐde Zhōngwén	shi	zài (at) nǎr (where)	xué (learn)	de?	Where did you learn Chinese? (implied past tense)
Wǒde Zhōngwén		zài (at) Niǔ Yuē	xué (learn)	de.	I learned Chinese in New York.

1) *Where* did you buy your clothes?	2) I bought them from Macy's.

CHAPTER 8: CULTURE-SPECIFIC CHINESE WORDS & PHRASES

Answer: 1) Nǐ **shì** *zài nǎr* <u>mǎi **de**</u> nǐde yīfú (clothes)?   2) Wǒ **shì** cóng Macy's mǎi **de**.

de (to introduce the result of a verb)

| s. | verb | | | result adv. | |
	v.	de	[neg.]	result adj.	English
Tā	zǒu (walk)			kuài (fast).	He walks fast.
Tā Zhōngwén	shuō (speak)			hǎo (good).	He speaks Chinese well.
Tā qí (chess)	xià (play chess)	de	[bu]	hǎo (good).	He plays chess well.
Tā	qǐ (get up)			zǎo (early).	He gets up early.
Wǒde gǎnmào (cold)	hǎo (better)			duō (much) le.	My cold is much better.
Tiānqì (The weather)	hǎo (good)	de		bùdeliǎo (extraordinary).	The weather is extraordinarily good.
Dōngxi (stuff)	guì (expensive)				The stuff is extraordinarily expensive.
Tiānqì (The weather)	hǎo (good)	de		*wǒ xiǎng qù sànbù.*	The weather is **so good that** *I want to go for a walk.*
Dōngxi (stuff)	guì (expensive)	de		*wǒ bù xiǎng zài mǎi le.*	The stuff is **so expensive that** *I don't want to buy further.*

1) The weather is <u>*extraordinarily* cold.</u>	2) The price is **so** cheap **that** I want to <u>buy more.</u>

Answer: 1) Tiānqì lěng **de** *bùdeliǎo*.   2) Jiàqián piányi **de** wǒ xiǎng <u>duō mǎi.</u>

de (to introduce the ability of carrying out the verb)

| s. | verb | | | result adverb | |
	v.	de	[neg.]	result verb	English (broken)
Wǒ	ná (pick)			qǐ (up).	I pick and am [not] able to get it up.
	zǒu (walk)			dòng (move).	I walk and am [not] able to move.
	kàn (look)	de	[bu] (drop de)	jiàn (see).	I look and am [not] able to see.
	lái (come)			jí (in time).	I come and am [not] able to be in time.
	tīng (listen)			dǒng (understand).	I listen and am [not] able to understand.
	mǎi (buy)			qǐ (afford).	I buy and am [not] able to afford.
	chī (eat)			wán (finish).	I eat and am [not] able to finish it.

1) I can hear it.	
2) I can finish (wán) this watermelon.	3) I am able to afford this car.
	4) It is thundering, so we are not able to *leave*.

Answer: 1) Wǒ tīng **de** dào/jiàn. 2) Wǒ chī **de** wán zhè ge xīguā. 3) Wǒ mǎi **de** qǐ zhè bù (unit) chē. 4) Tiān zài dǎléi, yīncǐ wǒmen zǒu **bù** lǎo (lǎo: result adj., able) le.

děi = must

s.	time adv.	v ₁	v ₂	the rest of the sentence	English
Wǒ	xiànzài (now)	děi	qù (go to)	shàngkè (class) le!	I must go to class now.
			zǒu/qù (go)	le.	I must go now.

1) It's too late, and I **must** go.	
2) I **must** pay my bills.	3) I **got to** go.

Answer: 1) Tài wǎn le, wǒ **děi** zuǒ le. 2) Wǒ **děi** fù wǒde zhàngdān. 3) Wǒ **děi** zuǒ le.

dōngxi = stuff, thingumajig

s.	adv.	v.	adj.	n.	English
Wǒ	chūqù (go out)	mǎi (buy)	[yì]diǎnr (some)	**dōngxi** (stuff).	I go out to buy some stuff.
Tā	bú	shì	zhēn (really)	[yīge] **dōngxi** (normal person)!	He is abnormal. He is a moron.

1) Is this your **stuff**?	2) Pick up your **stuff**, and let's go.

Answer: 1) Zhè shì nǐde **dōngxi** ma? 2) Ná qǐ nǐde **dōngxi**, wǒmen zǒu ba.

CHAPTER 8: CULTURE-SPECIFIC CHINESE WORDS & PHRASES

dōu = all, at all

s.	adv. (emphatic)	v.	obj.	English
Wǒmen (We)	dōu (all)	yǒu (have)	hùzhào (passports).	We **all** have passports.
		xiě (write)	ruǎnjiàn (software).	We **all** write software.
Wǒ (I)		yào (want).		I want them **all**.
		chī (eat).		I am able to eat **all** kinds of food.

obj.	adv. (emphatic)	v.	obj.	English
Yidiǎnr (A bit)	dōu (at all)	méi yǒu (don't have).		Don't have a bit **at all**. = Not at all.
		bù chī (don't eat)	ròu (meat).	Don't eat meat **at all**.

			v.	obj.	English
bù	dōu	—	yǒu (have)	hùzhào (passports).	Not **all** of us have passports.
—	dōu	méi			We **all** don't have passports.
bù	dōu	—	shì (are)	Měiguórén (Americans).	Not **all** of us are Americans.
—	dōu	bù			We **all** are not Americans.
bù	dōu	—	xiě (write)	ruǎnjiàn (software).	Not **all** of us write software.
—	dōu	bú			We **all** don't write software.

(Wǒmen (We))

s.	adv. (emphatic)	v ₁	v ₂	English
Wǒmen (We)	dōu	méiyǒu (didn't)	qù (go).	We **all** didn't go. None went.

s.	adv.	adj.	English
Tā	dōu (all)	xíng (good at).	He is a 'Jack of **all** trades'.
	Dōu (All)	kéyǐ/hǎo (okay/good).	**All** are okay/good.

s.	adv.	adj.		n.	the rest of the sentence	English
Nǐ	suǒ (inclusively)	shuō (say)	de	[huà (words)]	wǒ **dōu** (all) tīng (listen) dǒng (understood) le.	I understood **all** you said.

1) We **all** are American.

2) You **all** are correct.

3) We **all** are back.

4) About math and science, he is good at both.

Answer: 1) Wǒmen **dōu** shì Měiguórén.   2) Nǐmen **dōu** duì.   3) Wǒmen **dōu** huílai le.   4) Guānyú sùxüé hé kēxüé, tā **dōu** <u>xíng</u>.

duì = verb: correct

s.	v. 'to be'	[neg.]	adj.	English
Nǐ	shì (are)	[bú (not)]	**duì** (correct) .	You are [not] **correct**.

s.	v.	de	result	English
Nǐ	shuō (say)	de	**duì** (correct) .	What you say is [not] **correct**.

duì = verb: treat

s.	v.	obj.	the rest of the sentence	English
Tā	**duì** (treat)	nǐ	hěn (very) hǎo (good).	He treats you very well.

s.	v.	de	result	obj.	English
Tā	**duì** (treat)	de	qǐ (up to norm)	nǐ.	He treats you up to norm.
	duì (treat)	—	bù (not) qǐ (up to norm)		He treats you not up to norm. (= He offended you.)
	Duì (treat)	—	bù (not) qǐ (up to norm).		Excuse me. (= Sorry for I offended you.)

duì = preposition: to / toward

A	to	B	v.	obj.	English				
Yùndòng (Exercise)		nǐde shēntǐ (body)		bāngzhù (help).	Exercise,		your body,		help.
Wǒ	**duì**	Tā	yǒu (have)	xìngqù (interest).	I,	to	her,	has/	interest.
Wǒ		gāo'ěrfū		xìngqù (interest).	I,		golf,	have	interest.
Tā		nǐ		hǎocù (benefit).	It,		you,		benefit.

A	toward	B	de	n.	v.	inter. pronoun	English
Nǐ	—	—	de	kànfǎ (viewpoint)	shi	shénme?	What is your viewpoint?
Nǐ	**duì**	*nǎjiàn shiqíng*	de	kànfǎ (viewpoint)	shi	shénme?	What is your viewpoint **toward** *that matter?*
Nǐ	**duì**	tā	de	yìngxiàng (impression)	shi	shénme?	What is your impression **toward** him?

CHAPTER 8: CULTURE-SPECIFIC CHINESE WORDS & PHRASES

Nǐ	duì	tā	de	yǐngxiǎng (impression)	[shì]	zhěnmeyàng?	What is your impression **toward** him?

			v.	the rest of the sentence	English
A	**to**	B	shuō (speak/talk/tell)	C de mìmì (secret).	A speaks/talks/tells **to** B about C's secret.
A	**duì**	B			

Exercise

1) It might be **incorrect**.	3) *The boss* is speaking **to** us.
2) My boyfriend **treats** me very well.	4) He explains **to** me his <u>plan</u>.

Answer: 1) Kěnéng **búduì**. 2) Wǒde nánpéngyou **duì** wǒ hěn hǎo. 3) *Lǎobǎn* zāi **duì** wǒmen shuōhuà (speak). 4) Tā **duì** (to) wǒ shuōmíng (explain) <u>tāde jìhuà</u>.

duō = how (a question word)

s.	v.	inter. adv.	adj.	English
Nǐde (your) fángzi (house)			dà (big)	How big is your house?
Zhèxiē (These) xiàngmù (project)	yǒu (has)	*duō* (how)	nán (difficult)	How difficult are these projects? ?
Niǔ Yuē lí (apart from) Shànghǎi			yuǎn (far)	How far is it between New York and Shanghai?
Zhè zhī (unit) zhū (pig)			zhòng (heavy)	How heavy is the pig?

s.	v.₁	v.₂	inter. adv.	adj.	English
Nǐ	yào (will)	<u>qù</u> (be there)	*duō* (how)	jiǔ (long)	How long will you <u>be there</u>? ?
	xūyào (need)	—	(how)		How long (time) do you need?

duō = adjective: much/many; more; noun: '... and change'

s.	time adv.	v.	adj.	the rest of the sentence	English
Wǒmen	jīntiān (today)	yǒu (have)	hěn **duō** (much) de	gōngzuò (work).	Today we have lots of work.
Nǐ	—		**duōshǎo** (how much)	qián (money)?	**How much** money do you have?

s.	v.	n.	the rest of the sentence	English

s.	v.		duō (and change)	English
			. (only for single digit amount)	
Wǒ	yǒu (have)	liǎng (2) kuài	duō (and change)	I have 2 dollars and change.
		liǎng bǎi (200)	kuài.	I have 200 dollars and change.

adv.	adj.	the rest	English
Tài (too)	duō (much)	le! Gòu (enough) le! Xièxie.	Too much! Enough! Thanks.

adv.	v.	adv.	the rest	English
Shǎo (less)	shuō (talk),	duō (more)	tīng (listen) / zuò (do).	Talk less, listen/do more.

s.	perfect tense ind.	v.	de	result adj.	the rest	English
Wǒmen	yǐjīng (have)	zuò (do)	de	chā bù duō (differ not much to the target)	le.	We are almost there.

Exercise

1) **How** difficult is this project?   2) **How** tall are you?   3) I only have 20 dollars and change.

Answer: 1) Zhège xiàngmù yǒu duō nán?   2) Nǐ yǒu duō gāo?   3) Wǒ zǐ yǒu èrshí duō kuài.

gǎo = (informal) verb: engage in, do, make   synonym: gǎo = gàn

s.	progressive	v.	the rest	English
Wǒ		gǎo (engage in)	jiàoyù (education) gōngzuò (work).	I'm in education line of work.
Nǐ	zài	gǎo (do)	shěnme?	What are you doing?
Wǒ	zài	zuò (make)	dàngāo (cake).	I'm making a cake.

gěi = verb: give

s.	v.	obj.	the rest of the sentence	English
Tā	gěi (give) le	wǒ (me)	yī jiàn (unit) lǐwù (gift).	He gave me a gift.
Qǐng (Please)	gěi (give)	wǒ (me)	nèi (that) běn (unit) shū (book) hǎo ma?	Please give me that book?

CHAPTER 8: CULTURE-SPECIFIC CHINESE WORDS & PHRASES

gěi ... lái = verb: give (ordering food or drink)

s.	v.	obj.	prep.	the rest of the sentence	English
Qǐng (Please)	gěi (give)	wǒ (me)	lái (come)	yì píng (a bottle of) pijiǔ (beer).	Please give me a [bottle of] beer.

gěi = preposition: for

s.	v.	prep.	obj.	the rest of the sentence	English
Wǒmen	jìhuà (plan)	gěi (for)	tā	bàn (throw) yíge shēngrì qìngzhùhuì.	We plan to throw a birthday party for her.

s.	prep.	obj.	v.	obj.	the rest	English
	Gěi (For)	wǒ	jìn (go into)	nǐde (your)	fángjiān (room)!	Go to your room [for me]!
Tā	gěi (for)	wǒ	dǎ le	yíge diànhuà	.	He called me. (Note: This is a fixed format.)

s.	v.	obj.	prep.	obj.	English
Tā	dǎ le	yíge diànhuà	gěi (for)	wǒ (me).	He called me. (Note: This is a fixed format)

gěi = preposition: to

s.	v.	obj.	v.	prep.	obj.	the rest	English
Wǒ	bǎ	wǒde chuán (boat)	jiè (lend)	gěi (to)	tā		I lend my boat to him.
Tā		chuán (boat)	huán (return)	gěi (to)	wǒ	le.	He returns the boat to me.

Exercise

1) Please give me several days?

2) Please give me a bowl of chaomian. (ordering food)

3) Please call me.

4) I submitted my homework to the teacher.

Answer: 1) Qǐng gěi wǒ jǐ tiān hǎo mā? 2) Qǐng gěi wǒ lái yì wǎnr chǎomiàn. 3) Qǐng gěi wǒ dǎ yíge diànhuà. 4) Wǒ bǎ wǒde zuòyè jiāo gěi lǎoshī le.

gēn = verb: follow

Imperative	v	obj.	prep.	English

Qǐng (Please)	gēn (follow)	obj.	v₁		English
		wǒ (me)	lái (come).		Please follow me. (coming toward speaker)
		tā (he/she)	qù (go).		Please follow him/her. (away from speaker)
		wǒ (me)	niàn (read out loud).		Please read out loud after me.

gēn = preposition: to

s.		prep.	obj.	v₂		English
wǒ	néng	gēn (to)	Wáng xiānsheng	jiǎnghuà (speak)	ma?	May I speak to Mr. Wang?

s.	progressive	prep.	obj.	v.	English
wǒ	zài	gēn (to)	Wáng xiānsheng	jiǎnghuà (speak).	I'm speaking to Mr. Wang.

s.	prep.	obj.	v.		English
Tā	gēn (to)	wǒ	jiè (borrow)	qián (money).	He to me to borrow money. = He borrows money from me.
	gēn (to)	wǒ	dàoqiàn (apologize).		He to me to apologize. = He apologizes to me.

gēn ... [zài] yìqǐ = with (as in 'with someone')

s.	prep.	obj.		v.	the rest	English
Tā	gēn (with)	wǒ	[zài yìqǐ] (together)		.	She is with me.
	gēn (with)	wǒ	[zài yìqǐ] (together)	gōngzuò (work)	.	She works with me.
	gēn (with)	tāde (her) fùmǔ (parents)	[zài yìqǐ] (together)	zhù (live)	.	She lives with her parents.
	gēn (with)	wǒ	[zài yìqǐ] (together)	qù (go to)	Shànghǎi.	She goes to Shanghai with me.

A gēn B yíyàng adj. = A as adj. as B

	A	gēn	B	yíyàng	adj.	English
	Niǔ Yuē	gēn	Shànghǎi	yíyàng	dà.	New York is as big as Shanghai.

Exercise

1) Please sing with me.   2) He dines with me.   3) May I talk/speak with you?

Answer: 1) Qǐng gēn wǒ yìqǐ chàng.   2) Tā gēn wǒ yìqǐ chīfàn.   3) Wǒ néng gēn nǐ shuōhuà ma?

CHAPTER 8: CULTURE-SPECIFIC CHINESE WORDS & PHRASES

gèng = more; A bǐ B gèng adjective = A is more adjective than B

A	than (v.)	B	more	adjective	English
Júzi (orange)	bǐ	píngguǒ (apple)	gèng	tián (sweet).	Orange is sweeter than apple.
Wode (My) chē (car)	bǐ	tāde (his) chē	gèng	xiǎo (small).	My car is smaller than his car.
Nǐ		wǒ	gèng	adjective.	You are more adjective than I.
Nǐde		wǒde	gèng	adjective.	Your ... is more adjective than my ...

Exercise

1) His car is faster *than* mine.	2) Our product is **more** reliable *than* theirs.	3) This method is **better** *than* that method.

Answer: 1) Tāde chē **bǐ** wǒde [chē] **gèng** kuài.   2) Wǒmen de chǎnpǐn **bǐ** tāmen de [chǎnpǐn] **gèng** kěkào.   3) Zhège fāngfǎ **bǐ** nàge fāngfǎ **gèng** hǎo (more good = better — broken English is good Chinese).

guò = (1) verb: live through; (2) a perfect tense tag (see Chapter 6)

s.	v.	de	v.	result	English
Nǐde (Your) Gǎn'ēnjié (Thanksgiving)	guò	de		zěnmeyàng (how)?	How was (=How did you live through) your Thanksgiving?
Wǒde (My) Gǎn'ēnjié		de	bù	zěnmeyàng.	My Thanksgiving was not good.

hái = still, yet

s.	adv.	v.	adj.	obj.	English
Tāde chéngjī (grade)	hái (still)	shì (is)	bù hǎo (not good)	.	His grade still is not good.
Nǐ	hái (still)	yǒu méi yǒu (have or not have)		qián (money)?	Do you still have money?
Wǒ		yǒu (have)		yīxiē (some).	I still have some.
Wǒ	hái (still)	—	hǎo / kěyǐ / bú cuò	.	I'm still good/okay/not bad.

s.	adv.	v.	the rest of the sentence	English
Tā	—	lái le (came)	méi yǒu (or not)?	Did he come?
Nǐ	—	hǎo le (finished)		Are you finished?
	Hái (yet)	—	méi yǒu (not).	Not yet.

1) Do you **still want** to go?	2) He **still has** *hope* to win.	3) He <u>has</u> not come **yet**.

Answer: 1) Nǐ **hái** yào qù ma? 2) Tā **hái** yǒu *xīwàng* yíng. 3) Tā **hái** <u>méi</u> yǒu lái.

hǎo = adj.: good; v.: good; adv.: very, pleasant; result adv.: finish

s.	v.	number/unit	adj.	n.	English
Tā	shì (is)	[yíge]	**hǎo** (good)	rén (person).	She is a good person.

s.	v.		the rest	English
Nǐ	**hǎo** (verb 'good')		.	You good. = Hello.
Nǐ			ma?	You good? = How are you?
Nǐ[de] tàitai			ma?	Your wife good? = How is your wife?

s.	linking v.	[adv.]	v.	English
Zhèduǒ huā (flower)	smells (wénqǐlái)	[**hǎo** (= hěn, very)]	xiāng (aromatic).	This flower smells [very] aromatic.
Zhège píngguǒ (apple)	tastes (chángqǐlái)		tián (sweet).	This apple tastes [very] sweet.

s.	[adv.]	adv.	v.	English
Nǐde shēngyīn (voice)	[hěn (very)]	**hǎo** (pleasant)	tīng (listen).	Your voice is pleasant [to listen to].
Zhège píngguǒ (apple)			chī (eat).	This apple is delicious [to eat].
Zhège diànyǐng (movie)			kàn (watch).	This movie is fun [to watch].

s.	v.	result adv.	the rest	English
Wǒ	chī (eat)	**hǎo** (=wán, finish)	le.	I finished eating.
Wǒ	zuò (do)		le.	I finished [doing].

hào = crazy about

s.	adv.	v.	the rest	English
Tā	**hào** (crazy about)	chī (eat)	.	He is crazy about eating.

CHAPTER 8: CULTURE-SPECIFIC CHINESE WORDS & PHRASES

1) This toy is really fun to play.	2) Pulling tooth is very painful.	3) He is **crazy about** drinking.

Answer: 1) Zhège wánjù zhēn **hǎo wánr**. 2) Bá yá **hǎo téng/tòng**. 3) Tā **hào** hē jiǔ.

huí lái = return, back; huí jiā = return/back/go/get home

s.	inter. adv.	v₁	v₂	obj.	English
Nǐ	shénme shíhòu (when)	huì (will)	huí lái (return)		When will you return?
			huí lái (back)		When will you be back?
			huí (back/return)	jiā (home)	When will you be back/return home?
			dào (arrive)	jiā (home)	When will you arrive home?
			zài (at)	jiā (home)	When will you be [at] home?

s.	v. 'to be'	v₂ (verb phrase)	English
Wǒ	huì (shall) —	huí lái (back).	I shall be back.

s.	v₁	v₂	obj.	English
Wǒ	xiǎng / yào (want)	huí (go/return)	jiā (home).	I want to go home.

huì = know how to

s.	neg.	v₁	v₂	the rest	English
Nǐ		huì (know how to)	kāichē (drive a car)	ma?	Do you [know how to] drive?
Wǒ	—		kāichē	.	I [know how to] drive.
Nǐ			shuō (speak)	Yīngwén ma?	Do you [know how to] speak English?
Wǒ	bú (don't)		shuō	Yīngwén.	I don't [know how to] speak English?

huì = will (pertaining to probability)

s.	inter. adv.	v₁	v₂	v₃	the rest	English
Wǒ	míngtiān (tomorrow)	huì	qù (go to)	dǎ (play)	lánqiú (basketball).	I **probably will** go to play basketball tomorrow.

s.	adv.	v₁	v₂	English
	yídìng (certainly)			She certainly will come tomorrow. (most probable)
Tā	—	**huì**	lái (come).	She will come tomorrow. (good probability)
	míngtiān			
	kěnéng / dàgài / yěxǔ			She probably will come tomorrow. (less probable)

Exercise

1) Do you **know how** to fix a computer?	3) **Will** you *probably* go tomorrow?
2) I *probably* **will** <u>get</u> promoted *as* a manager.	

Answer: 1) Nǐ **huì** xiūlǐ diànnǎo ma? 2) Wǒ *kěnéng* **huì** <u>bèi</u> shēng *wéi* jīnglǐ. 3) Nǐ míngtiān *kěnéng* **huì** qù ma?

jiù (to stress the verb)   synonym: jiù = biàn

s.	emphatic adv.	v.	the rest of the sentence	English
Zhè (This)	jiù	shì (is)	wǒde (my) yìsi (point, meaning).	This **is** my point.

s.	emphatic adv.	v₁	v₂	the rest	English
Tiān (Sky)	jiù	yào (will)	xiàyǔ (rain)	le.	It will rain **at any moment.**
Tā			lái (arrive)	le.	He will arrive **at any moment.**

s.	v₁	emphatic adv.	v₂	English
Wǒ	qù qù (go away for a moment)	jiù	lái (come back).	I'll be **right** back.

s.	time adv.	emphatic adv.	v.	English
Wǒ	zǎoshàng (morning) wǔ diǎn (five o'clock)	jiù	xǐng (wake up) le.	I woke up **as early as** 5 o'clock this morning.

s.	emphatic adv.	v₁	v₂	obj.	English
Tā	jiù	ài (love)	chī (eat)	shǔtiáo (French Fries)	He **just** loves to eat French Fries.

yī ... jiù = as soon as   synonym: jiù = biàn

s.	adv.	v. phrase	adv.	v₁	v₂	the rest	English
Tā	yī	huí (return) jiā (home)	jiù	qù (go to)	kàn (watch)	diànshi (TV).	**As soon as** he returns home, he goes to watch TV.

Exercise

CHAPTER 8: CULTURE-SPECIFIC CHINESE WORDS & PHRASES

1) It **is** I.	3) I came at **as early as** 7 o'clock.
2) I **will leave as soon as** I *finish this call.*	4) I **will** become a father **at any moment.**

Answer: 1) **Jiù shì wǒ.** 2) Wǒ yī dǎ wán zhège diànhuà jiù yào zǒu. 3) Wǒ qī diǎn **jiù** lái le. 4) Wǒ **jiù yào** chéngwéi yíge fùqīng le.

kàn = short range view: watch/see/read/look; visit

s.	neg.	v.	obj.	English
Wǒ (I)	—	kàn (watch)	diànshì (TV) / diànyǐng (movie).	I watch TV/movie.
	—	kàn (see)	yīshēng (a doctor).	I see a doctor.
	—	kàn (read)	shū (book).	I read a book.
—	Bié (Don't)	kàn (look)	wǒ (me)!	Don't look at me!

s.	adv. phrase	v.	obj.	English
Wǒ (I)	*xiǎng qù yīyuàn*	kàn (visit)	*yíge péngyou.*	*I want to go to the hospital to visit a friend.*

s.	time adv.	v₁	v₂	v₃	the rest	English
Wǒ (I)	jīnwǎn (tonight)	néng (may)	*lái (come)*	kàn (visit)	nǐ ma?	May I come to visit you this evening?

kàn = long range view: see

s.	v.	result adv.	past tense tag	obj.	English
Wǒ (I)	kàn (see)	jiàn/dào	le	nǐde mèimei (younger sister).	I saw your sister.
				yìzhī dà zhōng xióng (a big brown bear).	I saw a big brown bear.

kàn = think - pertaining to expressing an opinion

s.	v.	clause			English
		yǒu (there exists)	wèntí (problem).		
Wǒ (I)	kàn (think)	zhège (this) dìfāng (place)	sìhū (seems)	bú (not) tài (quite) gǎnjìng (clean).	I think there is a problem.
					I think this place seems not quite clean.

120

Exercise

1) I'm **watching** TV. (short range)	3) I **saw** a UFO. (long range)
2) My parents <u>will come</u> to **visit** me this weekend.	4) I **think** we need to <u>change</u> direction.

Answer: 1) Wǒ zhèngzài **kàn** diànshì. 2) Zhège zhōumò wǒ bàmā (fùmǔ) <u>yào lái</u> **kàn** wǒ. 3) Wǒ **kàn jiàn/dào le** yíge UFO. 4) Wǒ **kàn** wǒmen xūyào gǎibiàn fāngxiàng.

kěyǐ = may, can   synonym: kěyǐ = néng

s.	time adv.	v ₁	v ₂	the rest	English
Wǒ	—	kěyǐ		ma?	May/Can I start?
Nǐ	xiànzài (now)		kāishǐ	le.	You may/can start now.

kěyǐ = good;   hái kěyǐ = so so

s.	v.	adj.	the rest	English
Nǐ	kàn (think)	kěyǐ (good)	ma?	What do you think?
Wǒ			le.	I think it's good.

Exercise

1) **Can** I take a week <u>vacation</u>?	2) That movie was **so so**.

Answer: 1) Wǒ **kěyǐ** qǐng yíge xīngqī de <u>jià[qī]</u> ma? 2) Nàge diànyǐng **hái kěyǐ**.

kuài = soon; hurry

s.	adv.	v ₁	v ₂	the rest	English
Tiān (Sky)	kuài (soon)	yào (will)	liàng (bright)	le.	The sky will soon be bright.
Wǒ	kuài (soon)	yào (will)	qù (go to)	Zhōngguó (China) le.	Soon, I will go to China.
	jiù kuài (sooner)				I am about to

CHAPTER 8: CULTURE-SPECIFIC CHINESE WORDS & PHRASES

emphatic adv.	adv.	adv.	v.	English
jiù (soonest)				Very soon, I will
Kuài (Hurry)	bié (don't)	zhème (so)	shuō (say)!	Don't say so! = Don't mention it!
	qǐng (please)		jìn [lái] (come in)!	Hurry right in please! (stronger than just 'please' alone)

Exercise

1) My birthday is about to come.	2) I am about to go to a meeting.

Answer: 1) Wǒde shēngrì jiù kuài yào lái/dào le.   2) Wǒ jiù kuài yào qù yíge huìyì (=qù kāihuì) le.

lái = come, qù = go to; xiān = first, hòu = later

s.	v.	the rest	English
Lǎo Wáng	lái (come)	le.	Mr. Wang came/arrived. = Mr. Wang is here.

s.	v₁ (emphatic)	v₂	the rest	English
Wǒ	[lái (come)]	bāng (help)	nǐ.	I [come] to help you.
Wǒmén		xuéxí (study)	Pīnyīn.	Let's [come] to study Pīnyīn.

v.	obj.	prep.	the rest	English
Gěi (Give)	wǒ	lái (toward speaker)	yìpíng (a bottle of) píjiǔ (beer).	Give me a beer.

adv.	imperative mood	v.	prep.	English
Qǐng (Please)	bú yào (don't)	guò (over)	lái (toward speaker).	Please don't come over here.
			qù (away from speaker).	Please don't go over there.

s.	v.	prep.	English
Wǒ	shàng	qù (away from speaker).	I go up.
Nǐ	xià	lái (toward speaker).	You come down.

s.	v₁	v₂	obj.	English
Wǒmén	qù (go to)	chī (eat)	wǔfàn (lunch).	Let's go to lunch.
Wǒ		shàng (attend)	kè (class).	I go to class.

s.	adv.	v.	English
Tā	xiān (first)	dào (arrive).	He arrives first.
Wǒ	hòu (later)		I arrive later.

Exercise

1) We are going to the movies. Would you like to come?   2) Please **give** me a Chicken ChowMein. Thanks.

Answer: 1) Wǒmen yào qù (will go to) kàn diànyǐng. Nǐ xiǎng lái ma?   2) Qǐng **gěi** wǒ **lái** yí ge/wǎnr jī chǎomiàn. Xièxie.

lǎo = old; always, constantly

s.	v. to be	subject complement (n. phrase)	English
Nàge (That) **lǎo** (old) rén (man)	shì (is)	yíge dì èr cì (II) shìjiè (W) dàzhàn (W) de yīngxióng (hero).	That old man is a WWII hero.

s.	freq. adv.	v. to be	adj.	English
Tā	**lǎo** (always)	—	chídào (late).	He is always late.

Exercise

1) This route is **always** jammed.   2) How are you, Bill? (Bill is Mr. Wang's first name.)

Answer: 1) Zhè tiáo (unit) lù **lǎo** dǔsè (dǔchē).   2) Nǐ hǎo ma, **lǎo** Wáng?

le = past tense tag; emphatic tag - See Chapter 6 'Tenses'

lí = verb 'distance'

A		B		English
v₁	subject	**v₂**	the rest	English
Niǔ Yuē **lí**	Shànghǎi	**yǒu** (has)	duō (how) yuǎn (far)?	How far is it **from** New York **to** Shanghai.
Zhèlì (Here) (distance)	chāojí (super) shìchǎng (market)	(has)		How far is it **from** here **to** super market?

CHAPTER 8: CULTURE-SPECIFIC CHINESE WORDS & PHRASES

Zhèlǐ		yīyuàn (hospital)		sān lǐ (3 miles).	The distance **from** here **to** hospital is 3 miles.
A		B	—	hěn jìn (near).	The distance **from** A **to** B is very near.

1) How far is it from your house to school?

2) The distance between *my house* and *work place* is *not far.*

Answer: 1) <u>Nǐ jiā **lí** xuéxiào **yǒu** duō yuǎn?</u> 2) *Wǒ jiā **lí** gōngzuò de dìfang bù yuǎn.*

lián ... dōu = even

s.	adv.	adj.	adv.	the rest	English
Nǐ	**lián** (even)	yìdiǎnr (a bit)	**dōu** (emphatic)	zhīdào (know) ma ?	You don't know at all (even a little bit)?

	n. phrase		conj.		clause	
Zhème (Such a) jiǎndān de (simple) wèntí (question)			**lián** (even)	wǒ	**dōu** (emphatic)	huì (know how to).

1) Such a complex question, **even** an expert doesn't know how to answer it.

2) Such a simple question, **even** my chauffeur is able to answer it.

Answer: 1) zhème yíge fùzá de wèntí, **lián** zhuānjiā dōu bú <u>huì</u> huídá. 2) zhèyàng yíge jiǎndān de wèntí, **lián** wǒde sījī dōu néng huídá.

liǎng (adj.) vs. èr (n.) = 2

	s.	v.	adj.	unit	the rest of the sentence	English
Wǒ		yǒu (have)	**liǎng** (2)	zhī	māo (cat).	I have two cats.
Jīnnián (This year)		shì	**liǎng** (2)		qiān líng bā (2008) nián.	This year is 2008.
					èr líng líng bā (2008) nián.	
Wǒde diànhuà (telephone) hàomǎ (number)		shì			**èr** liù **èr** wǔ sì yī qī (2625417).	My phone number is 2625417.

1) Please give us **two** bowls of beef soup noodle.	2) I'm in room **702**.	3) I'm at **second floor**.

Answer: 1) Qǐng gěi wǒmen lái **liǎng** wǎnr niúròu tāng miàn.　2) Wǒ zài dì qī líng **èr** hào fáng[jiān].　3) Wǒ zài [dì] **èr** lóu.

mán = adverb: pretty　　　　　synonym: mán = tǐng

s.	shì	adv.	adj.	de	English
Wǒ	[shì]	mán	hǎo (good)	de.	I'm **pretty** good.
Dōngxi (stuff)			guì (expensive)		The stuff is **pretty** expensive.

1) This stuff (food) is **pretty** delicious.	2) This movie is **pretty** entertaining.

Answer: 1) Zhège dōngxi **mán** hǎo chī de.　2) Zhège diànyǐng **mán** hǎo kàn de.

nán = adjective: difficult;　adverb: not good = bù hǎo

s.	v. to be	adv.	adj.	the rest of the sentence
Speaking English	is	very	difficult	.
Shuō (Speak) Yīngwén (English)	—	hěn	nán	.

s.	v. to be	adv.	adj.	v.	English
This movie	is	not	good.		This movie is lousy.
Zhège diànyǐng	—	bù	hǎo / nán	kàn (watch).	
This ice cream	is	not	good.		This ice cream tastes bad.
Zhège bīng qílín	—	bù	hǎo / nán	chī (eat).	

CHAPTER 8: CULTURE-SPECIFIC CHINESE WORDS & PHRASES

1) This dress is ugly.	2) This egg stinks.	3) That music sucks.

Answer: 1) Zhèjiàn yīfú **nán kàn**.   2) Zhège dàn **nán wén**.   3) Nàge yīnyuè **nán tīng**.

néng = can (allowed by permission) vs. huì (know how to)

s.	v₁	v₂	the rest	English
Nǐ	**néng** (can)	kāichē (drive a car)	ma?	Can you drive a car? (legal or sober enough)
Wǒ			.	I can drive.

1) Do you [**know how to**] drive?	2) Do you [**know how to**] speak English?	3) **Can** I fish here?

Answer: 1) Nǐ **huì** kāi chē ma?   2) Nǐ **huì** shuō Yīngwén ma?   3) Wǒ **néng** zài zhèlǐ diàoyú ma?

nòng = do, tackle, manage

s.	v₁	v₂	the rest	English
Wǒ	lái	**nòng** (do)	.	Let me **do** it.
Nǐ	huì bú huì	**nòng** (do)	?	Do you know how to **do** it?
Wǒ	bú huì	**nòng** (do)	.	I don't know how to **do** it.

1) You **broke** it.	2) I can **fix** it.	3) I can't **fix** it.

Answer: 1) Nǐ bǎ tā **nòng huài** le.   2) Wǒ néng **nòng hǎo** tā.   3) Wǒ bù néng **nòng hǎo** tā. = Wǒ **nòng** bù hǎo tā.

qǐng = adverb: please

adv.	v.	obj.		English
Qǐng (Please)	hē (drink)	chá (tea).		Please have some tea.

qǐng = verb: to invite someone as a guest

s.	v.	obj.	the rest	English
Wǒ	qǐng (invite)	nǐ	chī wǎnfàn (eat dinner).	I buy you dinner.
			kàn diànyǐng (watch movie).	I take you to the movies.

s.	v.		the rest	English
Wǒ	qǐng|kè| (invite you as a guest)		.	I buy.

Exercise

1) **Please** quiet. (= Quiet please.)   2) **Please** come in.   3) He **buys** me lunch.   4) We **invited** her to our house for dinner.

Answer: 1) **Qǐng** ānjìng.   2) **Qǐng** jìn [lái].   3) Tā **qǐng** wǒ chī wǔfàn.   4) Wǒmen **qǐng le** tā dào wǒmen jiā chī wǎnfàn.

qítā = other, the rest of, anything else

s.	v.	adj.	the rest	English
Nǐ	yǒu (have)	qítā de (other)	wèntí (questions) ma?	Do you have other questions?

Exercise

1) **Other** people are [all] gone for the day.   2) Where is the **other** document?   3) Do you have **anything else**?

Answer: 1) **Qítā** de rén dōu (emphatic) xiàbān le.   2) **Qítā** de wénjiàn zài nǎr?   3) Nǐ yǒu **qítā** de ma?

qù = verb: go to; preposition: to

s.	v₁	v₂	obj.	English
Tā	yào (will)	qù (go to)	Zhōngguó.	He will **go to** China.

s.	v.	prep.	obj.	English
Wǒmen (Let's)	zǒu (walk)	qù (to)	gōngyuán (park).	Let's walk **to** the park.

CHAPTER 8: CULTURE-SPECIFIC CHINESE WORDS & PHRASES

qù destination activity = go to/visit destination for activity

s.	time adv.	qù	place	activity	English
Wǒ	zuówǎn (last night)	qù le	tāde jiā (home/house)	wánr (fun).	I went his house [for fun] last night.
				chī wǎnfàn (dinner).	I went his house for dinner last night.

1) I will visit Paris next week.	2) We went to the lake **fishing** yesterday.

Answer: 1) Wǒ xià xīngqī yào **qù** Bālí **wánr**.   2) Wǒmen zuótiān **qù le** húbiān **diàoyú**.

shàng destination qù = go to destination   synonym: shàng = dào = wǎng

s.	v₁	v₂	destination	prep.	English
Wǒ	xiǎng (want)	shàng (go)	cèsuǒ (restroom)	qù (to).	I want to **go to** the restroom.
			chāojí shìchǎng (supermarket)		supermarket.
			túshūguǎn (library)		library.
Nǐ	xiǎng (want)	shàng (go)	nǎr (where)	qù (to)?	Where do you want to go?
	—	shàng (go)			Where are you going?

shuō = speak; shuōhuà = talk   synonym: shuō = jiǎng; shuōhuà = jiǎnghuà

s.	v₁	v₂	obj.	the rest	English
Nǐ	huì (know how to)	shuō	Zhōngwén	ma?	Do you [know how to] **speak** Chinese?

	adv.	adv.	v.	English
Xū (Shhh),	qǐng (please)	búyào (imperative 'do not')	shuōhuà (talk)!	Shhh … please do not **talk**! (Please be quiet!)

1) You **speak** English well.	2) Please *do not* **talk** during the class.

Answer: 1) Nǐ Yīngwén **shuō** dé hǎo.   2) Zài *shàngkè* de shíhòu qǐng *bú yào* **shuōhuà**.

suǒ = totally (emphatic usage)

s.	v. 'to be'	adj.		n.		English
Zhè (This)	shì	wǒ		qián (money)	de	This is my money.
Zhèxiē (These)	shì	wǒ	—	xìng (letters)		These are my letters.
			insert			
Zhè (This)	shì	wǒ	**suǒ** yǒu (have)	qián (money)	de	This is the money I [totally] have.
Zhèxiē (These)	shì	wǒ	**suǒ** xiě (write)	xìng (letters)		These are the letters I [totally] wrote.

	insert			n.	the rest of the sentence	English
Nǐ	**suǒ**	shuō (say)	de	huà (words)	wǒ dōu (all) tīng (listen) dǒng le (understood).	I understood the words you [totally] said.

Exercise

1) This is the stuff you [totally] **want**.   2) This is the <u>information</u> I [**totally**] **know**.

Answer: 1) Zhè shì nǐ **suǒ yào** de <u>dōngxī</u>.   2) Zhè shì **wǒ suǒ zhīdào** de <u>xiāoxí</u>.

tài = too, quite

s.	v. to be	adv.	adj.	the rest	English
[Nǐde dōngxi (stuff)]	~~shì (is)~~	**tài** (too)	guì (expensive)	le!	Your stuff is too expensive!
		Tài (too)	duō (much)	le!	Too much (wine, water, work, etc.)!
			hǎo (good)	le!	Excellent!
Tāde liǎn sè (facial expression)	bú (isn't)	**tài** (quite)	hǎokàn (pleasant)	.	His facial expression isn't quite pleasant.

Exercise

1) This dish is **too** <u>hot (spicy)</u>.   2) This place seems not **quite** clean.

Answer: 1) Zhè dào (unit) cài **tài** <u>là</u> le.   2) Zhè ge dìfāng sìhū bú **tài** gānjìng.

CHAPTER 8: CULTURE-SPECIFIC CHINESE WORDS & PHRASES

tì = verb: on behalf of, for

synonym: tì = dài

adv.	v₁	obj.	v₂	obj.	the rest	English
Qǐng	tì (on behalf of)	wǒ (me)	qù (go to)	kāihuì (meeting),	hǎo ma?	<u>Please</u> go to the meeting **for** (on behalf of) me?

Exercise

1) He <u>bought</u> a train ticket **for** me.

2) She *picked up* the guests **on behalf of** me *at the airport*.

Answer: 1) Tā tì wǒ <u>mǎi le yìzhāng huǒchē piào</u>.　2) Tā tì wǒ <u>zài fēijīchǎng</u> *jiē le kèrén*.

v. yī v. = v. v. kàn (give the verb a <u>try</u>) = v. yí xià (try the verb a moment)

adv.	v.	yī	v.	the rest of the sentence	English
Qǐng	cháng (taste)	yī (one)	cháng	zhè dào (unit) cài (dish).	Please taste this dish.
	mō (touch)		mō	zhè jiàn (unit) yīfú (dress) de zhìliào (material).	Please touch the material of this dress
	zuò (sit)		zuò	zhè bǎ (unit) yǐzi.	Please try sitting in this chair.

adv.	v.	kàn	the rest of the sentence	English
Qǐng	cháng (taste)	kàn (see)	zhè dào (unit) cài (dish).	Please taste this dish.
	mō (touch)		zhè jiàn (unit) yīfú (dress) de zhìliào (material).	Please touch the material of this dress.
	zuò (sit)		zhè bǎ (unit) yǐzi.	Please try sitting in this chair.

adv.	v.	yí xià	the rest of the sentence	English
Qǐng	cháng (taste)	yí xià (a moment)	zhè dào (unit) cài (dish).	Please taste this dish.
	mō (touch)		zhè jiàn (unit) yīfú (dress) de zhìliào (material).	Please touch the material of this dress.
	zuò (sit)		zhè bǎ (unit) yǐzi.	Please try sitting in this chair.

Exercise

1) Let me **taste** this grape.

2) May I test **drive** your new car?

Answer: 1) Ràng wǒ **cháng yi cháng** zhège pútao.　2) Wǒ kěyǐ **kāi yi kāi** nǐde xīn chē ma?

wán le = finished; have finished, a 'natural' perfect tense

s.	v.	adv.	the rest	English
Wǒ	chī (eat)	wán	le.	I have finished eating.
	kàn (read)			I have finished reading.
	zuò (do)			I have finished [doing].

1) I'm **finished**! (I'm in deep trouble!)	2) **Have you finished** [eating]?
3) We **have finished** playing <u>two basketball games</u>.	

Answer: 1) Wǒ **wán le**! 2) Nǐ chī **wán le** ma? 3) Wǒmen dǎ **wán le** <u>liǎng chǎng lánqiú bǐsài.</u>

wǎng = preposition: toward   synonym: wǎng = xiàng

prep.	n.	v.	obj.	the rest	English
Wǎng /Xiàng	dōng (east)	zǒu (walk)	100 mǐ	nǐ [jiù] huì (will) kànjiàn (see) dìtiě (subway).	Walking toward east 100 meters you'll see the subway.

1) <u>Go northward.</u>	2) <u>Drive southward.</u>	3) <u>Look westward.</u>

Answer: 1) **Wǎng** běi zǒu. 2) **Wǎng** nán kāi. 3) **Wǎng** xī kàn.   Note: 'Drive' (kāi) generally means to operate a machine.

wánr = play (non-sport), to have fun

s.	time adv.	adv.	v.	obj.	English
Wǒmen	zuówǎn	zài	**wánr** (play)	pái (cards).	We were playing cards last night.

adv.	freq. adv.	v 1	obj.	v 2	English
Qǐng	cháng (often)	lái (come to)	wǒ jiā (my house)	**wánr** (to have fun).	Please come to my house [to have fun] often.

130

CHAPTER 8: CULTURE-SPECIFIC CHINESE WORDS & PHRASES

1) Children are **play**ing hide-and-seek.	2) They are **play**ing basketball.	3) Come again [to have fun].

Answer: 1) Háizimen zài **wánr** zhuōmícáng.　2) Tāmen zài **dǎ** lánqiú.　3) Zài lái **wánr**.

wéi = preposition: as

s.	v.	obj.	prep.	obj.	English
Tāmen	xuǎn le (elected)	wǒ (me)	**wéi** (as)	xiàozhǎng (principal).	They elected me **as** the principal.

wèi le = because of, for

subject clause		v. to be	conj.	obj.	English
Tāmen	lái (come)	shi (is)	**wèi le** (because of)	nǐ.	They come (are coming) is because of you.
Nǐ	chídào (late)	shi (is)		shénme (what)?	Why are you late?

1) He joins our group **as** a consultant.	2) I work hard is **for** survival.

Answer: 1) Tā jiārù wǒmen [de] zhǔ **wéi** gùwèn.　2) Wǒ nǔlì gōngzuò shi **wèi** le shēngcún.

xiān …, zài … = … first, then …　　　　synonym: zài = hòu = ránhòu

s.		v.	obj.	first,	then	v.	obj.
We		eat	the appetizers	first (xiān),	then	[eat]	the main course.
Wǒmen	**xiān**	chī	kāiwèipǐn,		**zài**	chī	zhǔcài.

1) Let the elderly board the bus **first**, **then** the rest.	2) Measure **first**, cut **later**.

Answer: 1) Ràng lǎoniánrén **xiān** shàngchē, **zài** shàng qíyú de.　2) **Xiān** liáng, **zài** jiǎn.

xiǎng = think

aux.	s.	verb phrase			the rest	English
		xiǎng	**yì**	**xiǎng**		
Ràng (let)	wǒ (me)	xiǎng			.	Let me think about it.

xiǎng [yào] = want, would like, desire, contemplate/entertain the idea of

s.	v₁	v₂	the rest	English
Wǒ	xiǎng (want)	qù (go to)	Zhōngguó (China).	I want to go to China.

Exercise

1) I **want** to eat an ice cream. = I **would like** to eat an ice cream.	2) What do you **want** to *do* tonight?

Answer: 1) Wǒ **xiǎng** chī bīng qílín. 2) Jīnwǎn nǐ **xiǎng** *zuò* shénme?

yào = will (future tense)

s.	inter. adv.	v₁	v₂	obj.	English
Wǒ	—	yào (will)	qù (go to)	Zhōngguó (China).	I will go to China.
Nǐ	shénme shíhòu (when)	yào (will)	shàng (get on)	fēijī (airplane)?	When will you get on the plane? (=When is your flight?)

yào … le = be going to

s.	v₁	v₂	obj.	the rest	English
Wǒ	yào (am going to)	qù (go to)	Zhōngguó (China)	le.	I am going to go to China.
		zǒu (leave)	—	le.	I am going to leave. (= I'm leaving.)

yào = want (determined)

s.	v₁	obj.	v₂	obj.	English
Wǒ	yào (want)	jī (chicken).	—	—	I want chicken.
		—	chī (eat)	wǔfàn (lunch).	I want to eat lunch.

CHAPTER 8: CULTURE-SPECIFIC CHINESE WORDS & PHRASES

s.	v₁	obj.	v₂	obj.	English
Tā	yào (want)	nǐ (you)	zuò (do)	shénme (what)?	What does he want you to do?
Wǒde lǎobǎn (boss)		wǒ (me)	qù (go to)	kāihuì (meeting).	My boss wants me to go to a meeting.

Yào = Be; bú yào = imperative 'don't'

Be	adj.	English
Yào	xiǎoxīn (careful) / rěnnài (patient).	Be careful/patient.

imperative 'don't'	v.	English
Qǐng (Please)	bú yào	xīyān (smoke).
		Please do not smoke.

Exercise

1) I'm going to graduate.   2) I want to go to the movies.   3) I will play basketball tomorrow.   4) Please don't loiter.

Answer: 1) Wǒ yào bìyè le.   2) Wǒ yào qù kàn diànyǐng.   3) Wǒ míngtiān yào dǎ lánqiú.   4) Qǐng bú yào xiánguàng.

yě = also, too

s.	adv.	v₁	v₂	the rest of the sentence	English
Wǒ	yě (also)	xiǎng (desire, want)	qù (go to)	Zhōngguó (China).	I also want to go to China.
				2) I am an American too.	

Exercise

1) I also study Chinese.   2) I am an American too.

Answer: 1) Wǒ yě xuéxí Zhōngwén.   2) Wǒ yě shì [yíge] Měiguórén.

[yī]diǎnr = adverb: a little bit; adjective: some   synonym: [yī]diǎnr = [yī]xiē

s.	v.	adv.	the rest	English
		[yī]diǎnr	le ma?	Are you a little bit better?
Nǐ	hǎo (good)	duō (much)		Are you much better?

		[yī]diǎnr	le.	
Wǒ	hǎo (good)	duō (much)		I'm a little bit better.
				I'm much better.

s.	v.	adv.	the rest	
Qǐng (Please)	zǒu (walk)	kuài (fast) [yī]diǎnr	hǎo ma?	Walk a little bit faster, please?

s.	v.	le	adv.	the rest	English
Zhè tiáo (unit) kùzi (pants)	cháng (long)	le	[yī]diǎnr		This pants is a little bit long.
Zhè jiàn (unit) yīfú (dress)	dà (large)			.	This dress is a little bit large.

s.	adv.	v.	adj.	the rest	English
Wǒ	chūqù (go out)	mǎi (buy)	[yī]diǎnr (some)	dōngxi (stuff).	I go out to buy some stuff.

Exercise

1) A little bit this, a little bit that.   2) Could you speak a little bit slower?   3) Could you speak a little bit louder?

Answer: 1) **Yīdiǎnr** zhège, **yīdiǎnr** nàge.   2) Nǐ néng shuō <u>màn **yīdiǎnr**</u> ma?   3) Nǐ néng shuō <u>dàshēng **yīdiǎnr**</u> ma?

yīnggāi = should, ought to   synonym: yīnggāi = yīngdāng

s.	adv.	v₁	v₂	the rest	English
Nǐ	—	yīnggāi (should)	qù (go to)	shàngkè (class).	You should go to class.
			xuéxí (learn)	Zhōngwén (Chinese).	You should learn Chinese.
Wǒmen	dōu (all)		zuò (do)	yùdòng (exercise).	We all should do exercise.

Exercise

1) We **should** follow the rules.   2) We **ought to** be very careful.

Answer: 1) Wǒmen **yīnggāi** zūnshǒu guīzé.   2) Wǒmen **yīnggāi** fēicháng xiǎoxīn.

CHAPTER 8: CULTURE-SPECIFIC CHINESE WORDS & PHRASES

yìsi = meaning/point; intent; fun; etiquette; token

s.	v. to be		adj.	n.	English
'Méi yìsi'	shi (is)		'méiyǒu (no) qù (fun)' de	yìsi (meaning).	'Méi yìsi' means 'no fun'.
Nǐde yìsi (point)	shi (is)		—	shénme (what)?	What's your point? What do you mean by that?
Zhè (This)	jiù	shi (is)	wǒde (my)	yìsi (point).	This **is** my point. (jiù: emphatic)

s.	v. to be	adj.	n.	English
Zhè (This)	shi (is)	shénme (what)	yìsi (meaning)?	What does this mean? (a plain question)
Zhè (This)	shi (is)	shénme (what)	yìsi (meaning)?	*Angry tone:* What is this supposed to mean?!
Nǐ	shi (is)	shénme (what)	yìsi (intent)?	*Angry tone:* What are you trying to pull?

adv.	v.	n.	English
[Zhēn (Really)]	yǒu (have)	yìsi (fun)!	[Very] funny/interesting!

	adv.	adj.	n.	English
Duì bu qǐ (I'm sorry).				I'm sorry. I fall short in **etiquette**.
Xièxie nǐde bāngzù (help)! = Máfan (Trouble) nǐ le!	[Zhēn (Really)]	bù hǎo (no good)	yìsi (etiquette).	Thank you for your help! I fall short in **etiquette**.

adv.	adj.	n.	English
Yìdiǎnr (A little bit)	xiǎo (small)	yìsi (token).	Not much, a small token. (When you offer a gift to someone.)
A common response is: The short form is:		yìsi yìsi.	
Zhēn/Tài xièxie nǐ le! Nǐ tài (too) kèqi le!			Thank you so much! You are too kind!

Exercise

1) My **point** is that we were wrong.	2) No **fun** at all.	3) It **has** so *much* **fun**!	4) It is *so* **interesting**!

Answer: 1) Wǒde yìsi shi wǒmen cuò le.   2) Zhēn méi **yìsi**.   3) Tài **yǒu yìsi** le!   4) Tài **yǒu yìsi** le! (same as in 3)

yí xià = for a moment, briefly   synonym: yí xià = yì huǐr

v.	adv.	the rest	English
Qǐng ràng wǒ	wán (play)	yí xià	hǎo ma?	Let me play **for a moment please**?
[Ràng] wǒmen (Let's)	xiūxí (rest)	yí xià	.	Let's rest **for a moment**. (=Let's take a break.)

1) *Please* help me to <u>find</u> [**brief**] my cell phone?	2) Let's take a [**brief**] look at your plan.

Answer: 1) *Qǐng* bāng wǒ <u>zhǎo</u> **yí xià** wǒde shǒujī, *hǎo ma?* 2) Ràng wǒmen kàn **yí xià** nǐde jìhuà.

yòng = use

s.	v₁	v₂	obj.	English
Wǒ	<u>huì (know how to)</u>	yòng (use)	diànnǎo (computer).	I <u>know how to</u> use a computer.

yòng = with (as in 'with a tool')

s.	prep. phrase to specify the verb	v.	obj.	English
Tā	*yòng* mùgùn	dǎ (hit)	shé (snake).	He hits the snake *with* a stick.

1) Do you <u>know how to</u> **use** *a cell phone?*	2) I *wrote* a letter **with** a fountain pen.

Answer: 1) Nǐ <u>huì</u> **yòng** *shǒujī* ma? 2) Wǒ **yòng** gāng bǐ *xiě le* yì fēng (unit for letter) xìn.

yóu someone lái/qù = let (with a hint of entrusting) someone to do something

Yóu	someone	lái/qù	v.	the rest	English
Yóu	tā	lái/qù	lǐngdǎo (lead)	zhège (this) zǔ (team).	**Let him to lead** this team.
			bànyǎn (play)	zhège (this) jiǎosè (role).	**Let him to play** this role.

Yóu	someone	qù		the rest	English
Yóu	tā	qù (go)	ba!		Let him go and do whatever!

CHAPTER 8: CULTURE-SPECIFIC CHINESE WORDS & PHRASES

adv.	yǒu	someone	the rest	English
Dōu (All, emphatic)	yǒu	nǐ	le. (emphatic)	It's all up to you.

Exercise

1) **Assign** her **to** play Juliet's role.	2) **Assign** him **to** <u>be</u> the manager, we *have a peace of mind.*

Answer: 1) **Yóu tā lái** <u>yǎn</u> (v.) Juliet de jiǎosè.   1) **Yóu tā lái** <u>dāng</u> jīnlǐ, wǒmen *fàngxīn.*

yǒu = have

s.	v.	obj.	conj.	s.	v.	obj.	English
Wǒ	**yǒu** (have)	shíjiān (time),	dànshi (but)	wǒ	méi **yǒu** (don't have)	qián (money).	**I have** time, but I don't **have** money.

s.	v.	obj.	the rest	English
Nǐ	**yǒu** (have)	Yīngwén (English) míngzi (name)		Do you **have** an English name?
		kòng (spare time)	ma?	Do you **have** spare time?

yǒu (have) + noun = adj.

		adj.		English	
s.	adv. phrase	yǒu (have)	noun		adj.
Chī (Eating) shuǐguǒ (fruits)	<u>duì</u> (to) nǐde shēntǐ (body)	**yǒu**	bāngzhù (help).	Eating fruits is	helpful <u>to your body.</u>

			adj.				English	
s.	be	unit	yǒu (have)	noun	de	n.		adj.
Tā	shi	yíge	**yǒu**	quánlì (power)	de	rén.	He is a	powerful man.
				zhìhuì (wisdom)	de			wise

yǒu = there is/are/... = exist

v.	the rest of the sentence		English
Yǒu (There are)	hóng de, lán de, hé (and) bái de huā (flower)	ma?	**Are there** red, blue, and white flowers?
		.	**There are** red, blue, and white flowers.
	yāoguài	ma?	**Are there** monsters?

yǒu [yī]diǎnr = verb 'to be' + a little bit   synonym: [yī]diǎn = [yī]xiē

s.	v.	adv.	adj.	s.	v. 'to be'	a little bit	adj.
Wǒ	yǒu	[yī]diǎnr	lěng.	I	am	a little bit	cold.
Zhè tiáo (unit) kùzi (pants)			cháng (long).	This pants	are	a little bit	long.
Zhè jiàn (unit) yīfú (dress)			dà (large).	This dress	is	a little bit	large.

yǒu + a time frame = for a time frame

s.	aux.	v.	prep.	obj.	prep.	obj.
I	have	lived	in	New York City	for	many years.
Wǒ		yǐjīng zhù	zài	Niǔ Yuē Shì	yǒu	xǔduō nián [le].

Exercise

1) She is a trustworthy person.	2) **There are** *things* to eat and ride at the State Fair.	3) I have studied Chinese **for** five years.

Answer: 1) Tā shì yíge **yǒu** xìnyòng de rén.   2) Zài State Fair **yǒu** chī de hé wánr de *dōngxi*.   3) Wǒ yǐjīng xuéxí Zhōngwén **yǒu** wǔ nián [le].

yǒu de ..., yǒu de ..., yǒu de ..., = some ..., some ..., some ...,

prep. phrase	s.	v. phrase	s.	the rest
Among the students,	some	know how to drive,	some	don't know how to drive.
Zài xuéshēng lǐ	yǒu de	hui kāichē,	yǒu de	bú hui kāichē.
Among the choices,	some	are easy,	some	are difficult.
Zài xuǎnzhé lǐ	yǒu de	— róngyì,	yǒu de	— nán.

yòu (又) = undesirable 'again'

s.	adv.	v.	emphatic	English
Tā	yòu (again)	lái (come)	le.	He comes again.

CHAPTER 8: CULTURE-SPECIFIC CHINESE WORDS & PHRASES

yòu = also

s.	v.	adv.	adj.	adv.	adj.	English
Zhège píngguǒ	[shì] (is)	yòu (also)	dà (big),	yòu (also)	tián (sweet),	yòu (also)	duōzhī (juicy).	This apple is big, sweet, and juicy.

1) After the marathon, I am thirsty and tired. | 2) She types fast and well.

Answer: 1) Mǎlāsōng zhīhòu, wǒ yòu kě yòu lèi.   2) Tā dǎzì yòu kuài yòu hǎo.

yüè lái yüè adj. = getting more adj. and more adj.

s.	yüè lái yüè	adj.	English
Tā	yüè lái yüè (getting more and more)	piàoliang (pretty) [le].	She is getting prettier and prettier.

yüè v. yüè adj. = v. more adj. and more adj.

s.	yüè	v.	yüè	adj.	English
Nǐ	yüè (more)	zǒu (walk)	yüè (more)	kuài (fast).	You walk faster and faster.

yüè adj₁ yüè adj₂ = the more adj₁ the more adj₂

s.	yüè	adj₁.	yüè	adj₂.	English
	Yüè (more)	kuài (soon) / zǎo (early)	yüè (more)	hǎo (good).	The sooner the better. (As soon as possible.)
Zhùfú (blessing)	yüè (more)	duō (much)			Blessings are the more the better.

1) The weather is getting hotter and hotter. | 2) Vacation is the longer the better.

Answer: 1) Tiānqì yüè lái yüè rè [le].   2) Jiàqī yüè cháng yüè hǎo.

zài (在) = (1) prep: at/in/on/…;   (2) a verb 'at/in';   (3) progressive adverb

s.	v.	prep.	the rest of the sentence	English
Wǒ	zhù (live)	**zài** (in/at)	Niǔ Yuē Shì (New York City).	I live **in** New York City.
Wèishēngjiān (restroom)		**zài** (at)	nǎr (where)?	Where is the restroom?
Wáng xiānsheng		**zài** (in)	ma?	Is Mr. Wang **in**?

s.	v. + prep. (L)	n.	prep. (R)	English
Píngguǒ (apple)	**zài**	zhuōzi (table)	**shàng.**	Apple is **on** the table.
Zhuōzi (Table)	**zài**	fángjiān (room)	**lǐ.**	The table is **inside** the room.

s.	progressive adv.	v.	the rest of the sentence	English
Nǐ	**zài**	zuò (do)	shénme (what)?	What are you **doing**?

Exercise

1) Where were you last night?   2) I was **at** home *watching* TV.

Answer: 1) Nǐ zuówǎn **zài** nǎr?   2) Wǒ **zài** jiā *kàn* diànshì.

zài (再) = desirable 'again'

s.	adv.	v.			English
	Zài (again)	jiàn (see).			See **again**. (=good bye.)
		lái (come).			Come **again**.
Wǒmen	**zài** (again)	shì (try)	[yī]	shì.	Let's try **again**.

s.	adv.	v.	number	time	English
Wǒmen	**zài** (again)	shì (try)	yí (one)	cì (time).	Let's try **again** one time.

zài (再) = adverb: further

s.	aux.	adv.	v.	obj.	emphatic	English
Wǒ	bù néng	<u>zài</u> (further)	<u>jiǎn</u> (reduce)	jià (price)	le.	I can't reduce the price <u>further</u>.
			hē (drink)	—		I can't drink <u>further/anymore</u>.

CHAPTER 8: CULTURE-SPECIFIC CHINESE WORDS & PHRASES

zài (再) = conjunction: then

adv.	v.	obj.	conj.	v.	obj.	English
Xiān (First)	chī (eat)	fàn (rice),	zài (then)	hē (drink)	tāng (soup).	First eat rice, then drink soup.

adv.	v.	adv.	conj.	v.	adv.	English
Xiān (First)	liáng (measure)	liǎngcì (twice),	zài (then)	jiǎn (cut)	yícì (once).	First measure twice, then cut once.

s.	adv.	v.	conj.	v.	English
Wǒmen	xiūxi (rest)	yí xià (moment)	zài (then)	zǒu (walk).	Let's rest a moment then continue our walk.

1) He makes the *same* mistake **again and (over and over) again.**   2) I want to see that movie **again** *five times.*

Answer: 1) Tā **yí zài** fàn *tóngyàng de* cuòwù.   2) Wǒ yào **zài** kàn nàge diànyǐng *wǔ cì.*

v. + zhe (to emphasize the progressiveness)

s.	adv. phrase	v.	zhe	English		
Tā	zài yǐzi lǐ	zuò (sit)	zhe.	She	is sitting	in a chair.
Wǒde gǒu	zài sāfā shàng	shuì (sleep)		My dog	is sleeping	on the sofa.
Tā	zài chuáng shàng	tǎng (lie)		He	is lying	in bed.

s.	v₁	zhe	v₂	n. (obj.)	English
				verb phrase	
Tā	chī (eat)	zhe	jiǎng (talk)	huà (words).	He talks while eating.
Tā	zǒu (walk)	zhe	kàn (read)	shū (book).	He reads while walking.

1) Ducks are swimming *in the water.*   2) He sleeps while standing.

Answer: 1) Yāzimen **zài** suǐ lǐ yóu **zhe**.   2) Tā zhàn **zhe** shuì jiào.

zhème = adverb: so, such   synonym: zhème = nàme (used as an adverb)

s.	v.	adv.	adj.	n.	English
Nǐ	xūyào (need)	zhème (so)	duō (much) de	qián (money) ma?	Do you need **so** much money?
Wǒ	bù néng (can't) jiějué (solve)	zhème (such)	nán (difficult) de	wèntí (problem).	I'm not able to solve **such** a difficult problem.

nàme = conjunction: so then

conj.	s.	v.	the rest	English
...,	nàme (so then),	[ràng] wǒmen	xiūxí (rest) wǔ fēnzhōng	ba.	..., **so then**, let's rest for <u>five minutes</u>.

1) Are we able to <u>handle</u> **so** much business?   2) **So then**, what is <u>your point</u>?

Answer: 1) Wǒmen néng <u>chǔlǐ</u> **zhème** duō de shēngyì ma?   2) **Nàme**, <u>nǐde yìsi shì shénme?</u>

zhēn = adverb: so, really

s.	adv.	v₁	v₂	prep.	Obj.	English
Wǒ	zhēn (so)	gāoxìng (glad, pleased)	jiàn (see)	dào	nǐ.	I am **so** glad to see you.

s.	v.	adv. phrase			English
Nǐ Yīngwén	shuō (speak)	de	zhēn (really)	hǎo/bàng (good).	You speak English **really** well.

zhēn = adverb: really, so, very (placed at the beginning of a sentence to add emphasis)

adv.	v.	English
	tǎoyàn!	**Really/So/Very** annoying!
Zhēn	xiào (laugh) sǐ (to death) rén (people) le!	Positive: It's **really/so/very** funny! / Negative: It's ridiculous!
(Really/So/Very)	qì (angry) sǐ (to death) wǒ le!	It got me **really/so/very** angry/mad!
	piàoliang (pretty)!	**Really/So/Very** pretty!

zhēn de = adjective: real, really

CHAPTER 8: CULTURE-SPECIFIC CHINESE WORDS & PHRASES

s.	v. to be	adj.		the rest	English
Zhège yù (jade)	**shì** (is)	**zhēn** (real)	**de**	ma?	Is this jade real?
	Shì (is)	**zhēn**	**de**	.	It's real.
	Shì (is)	**zhēn**	**de**	ma?	Really?
	Shì (is)	**zhēn**	**de**	.	Yes, it's real.

1) Your house is **really/so** big.

2) This is a **real** jade.

Answer: 1) Nǐde fángzi **zhēn** dà.　2) Zhè shi yíge **zhēn de** yù.

zǒu = walk, leave, go

s.	v.	prep.	obj.	English
Wǒmen (We)	**zǒu** (walk)	qù (to)	gōngyuán (park).	We walk to the park.

s.	inter. adv.	prep.	v.	English
Nǐ	shénme shíhòu (when)	—	**zǒu** (leave). v_1	When do you leave?
Nǐ	shénme shíhòu (when)	yào (will)	**zǒu** (leave). v_2	When will you leave?

s.	v.	the rest	English
Wǒmen (Let's)	**zǒu** (go)	ba.	Let's go.
		ba?	Shall we go?

zuì = the most (superlative degree)

s.	v.	de (得)	adv. phrase / adj.		English
			adj.		
Nǐ Zhōngwén	shuō (speak)	de (得)	hǎo (good).		You speak Chinese well.
			adj. phrase		
Nǐ Zhōngwén	shuō (speak)	de (得)	**zuì** (the most)	hǎo (good).	You speak Chinese the best.

s.	v. to be	adj. phrase		n.	English
		zuì (the most)	xiān (early)		
Tā	shì (is)	zuì (the most)	xiān (early)	dàodá (arrive).	He is **the earliest** to arrive.

s.	adv.	adj.		the rest	n.	English
	zuì (the most)	dà (old)	de (的)			
Wǒde	zuì (the most)	dà (old)	de (的)	gēge (older brother)	shì (is) lǜshī (lawyer).	My **oldest** older brother is a lawyer.

s.	v.	n. phrase				English
		pí (naughty)	zuì (the most)	de (的)	yíge (one)	
Nàge (That) háizi (kid)	shì (is)	pí (naughty)	zuì (the most)	de (的)	yíge (one).	That kid is **the most naughty** one.

Exercise

1) He is the **best** student in the class.

2) He came in (arrived) **last**.

3) I don't like stinky tofu the **most**.

Answer: 1) Tā shì *bān shàng* zuì hǎo de xuésheng.　2) Tā zuì hòu dàodá.　3) Wǒ zuì bù xǐhuān chòu dòufu le.

zuò (坐) = sit;　zuò (坐) / dā (搭) / chéng (乘) = take (transportation)

s.	v.	prep.	obj.	the rest of the sentence	English
Wǒ	zuò (sit)	zài	yǐzi (chair)	shàng.	I sit on a chair.
Wǒ	zuò (take)	—	fēijī (airplane)	qù (go to) Shànghǎi.	I take airplane to go to Shanghai.

Exercise

1) I **sit** in a classroom.

2) I **take** train to Beijing.

3) What did you **take** to *come here*.

Answer: 1) Wǒ zuò zài jiàoshì lǐ.　2) Wǒ dā huǒchē qù Běijīng.　3) Nǐ dā le shénme lái zhèlǐ?

Appendix A

A Quick Reference for Handy Conversation Lines

A.1   Greetings

Vocabulary: morning (zǎo, zǎoshàng); noon (wǔ); evening/night (wǎn); peace (ān);
teacher (lǎoshī); y'all (dàjiā).

Initiation		Possible Response
English	**Chinese**	
Good morning.	Zǎo ān. = Zǎoshàng hǎo. = Zǎo.	Copy or pick one you prefer.
Good afternoon.	Wǔ ān (including noon).	Copy.
Good evening/night.	Wǎn ān. = Wǎnshàng hǎo.	Copy.
Good morning, _____.	<u>Lǎoshī</u> zǎo. <u>Dàjiā</u> zǎo.	Change the subject accordingly.

Vocabulary: a verb 'good/well' (hǎo); recently (jìnlái); very (hěn); excellent (hǎojíle, jí means extremely); too (tài); how is (zěnmeyàng); days (rìzi); not (bù); still (hái); not bad (hái hǎo); bad/wrong (cuò); fairly (tǐng/mán); busy (máng); weekend (zhōumò); blind (xiā); welcome (huānyíng).

Initiation		Possible Response
English	**Chinese**	
Hello.	Nǐ hǎo.	Copy.
How are you?	Nǐ hǎo ma?	Hǎo. / Hěn hǎo. / Hǎojíle. Nǐ ne (And you)? So so. = Māmǎhūhū. = Hái hǎo. Same old = not much = Lǎo yàngzi. Not bad. = [Hái] bú cuò. Pretty good. = Tǐng/Mán hǎo de.
How are you recently?	Nǐ jìnlái hǎo ma?	
What's up?	Nǐ zěnmeyàng?	
How have you been?	Nǐde rìzi zěnmeyàng?	
How's your life treating you?		
How's your weekend?	Nǐde zhōumò hǎo ma?	
Long time no see, how are you?	Hǎo jiǔ bú jiàn, nǐ hǎo ma?	
Are you busy?	Nǐ máng ma?	Bù/Hěn/Xiā máng. Tài máng le. Hái hǎo.
Hello, teacher <u>Guō</u>.	<u>Guō</u> lǎoshī hǎo.	Change the surname accordingly.
Welcome	Huānyíng.	Thank you (Xièxie nǐ).
Please say hello to ...	Qǐng wènhòu ...	Hǎo de, xièxie nǐ. (I will, thank you.)
Have you eaten?	[Nǐ] chī guò le méi yǒu?	Not yet. (Hái méi yǒu.) And you? (Nǐ ne?)
		I have. (Chī guò le.) Nǐ ne?

A.2   Polite words and phrases

Vocabulary: thank (xièxie); nín = a respectful nǐ; not (bú=bié); guest attitude (kè qì); no need (bú yòng); no (méi); problem (wèntí); matter (shì'er); concern (guānxi); ask (wèn); tell (gàosù); come in (jìn [lái]); sit (zuò); eat (chī); food in various dishes (cài); trouble (máfán); in advance (xiān).

Initiation		Possible Response
English	**Chinese**	
Thank you.	Xièxie nǐ/nín.	You're welcome. = Bú kè qì. = Bú yòng xiè. = Bú xiè.
Excuse me.	Duì bù qǐ.	No problem. = Méi wèntí. = Méi guānxi. = Méi shì'er.
May I ask ...	Qǐng wèn ...	Answer the question.
Please tell me ...	Qǐng gàosù wǒ ...	
Please come in.	Qǐng jìn〔lái〕.	Follow the offer and say 'xièxie'.
Please have a seat.	Qǐng zuò.	
Please have some tea.	Qǐng hē (drink) chá.	
Please eat.	Qǐng chī cài.	
Please wait.	Qǐng děng yì děng.	Méi wèntí. = No problem.
Sorry to trouble you.	Máfan nǐ le.	Bù máfán. = No trouble at all. = No problem.
Thanks in advance.	Xiān xièxie [nǐ] le.	Méi wèntí. = No problem. = You're welcome.
Thanks a lot!	Duō xiè [nǐ] le!	
What happened?	Zěnme le?	Nothing. = Méi shénme. Not too good. = Bú tài hǎo.

A.3   Let me buy you lunch.

Vocabulary: Let me = me = wǒ; buy = invite = qǐng; fàn = cooked rice = meal; to eat a meal = chī fàn; to drink coffee = hē kāfēi; etiquette (yìsi); bù hǎo yìsi = I fall short of etiquette; come to my house = dào wǒ jiā lái; have fun = wánr; What time? = Shénme shíhòu?

Initiation		Possible Response
English	**Chinese**	
Let me **buy** you a meal / cup of coffee.	Wǒ **qǐng** nǐ chī fàn / hē kāfēi.	1) Tài xièxie nǐ le. Bù hǎo yìsi (=You're very kind).
Let's go eat (a meal)! I **buy**.	Wǒmen qù chī fàn! Wǒ **qǐngkè**.	
I **buy** you dinner. = I **invite** you to eat dinner.	Wǒ **qǐng** nǐ chī wǎnfàn.	2) Bù, wǒ **qǐngkè**.
I would like to **invite** you to my house for dinner.	Wǒ xiǎng **qǐng** nǐ dào wǒ jiā lái chī wǎnfàn.	Tài xièxie nǐ le. Shénme shíhòu? (What time?)

Meal = fàn (literally: cooked rice)   to eat a meal = chī fàn
Breakfast = morning (zǎo) meal (fàn) = zǎofàn;   to eat breakfast = chī zǎofàn
Lunch = noon (wǔ) meal (fàn) = wǔfàn;   to eat lunch = chī wǔfàn
Dinner = evening (wǎn) meal (fàn) = wǎnfàn;   to eat dinner = chī wǎnfàn

A.4   What's your name?

Vocabulary: expensive / honorable (guì); surname (xìng, a verb); I'm called (wǒ jiào); business card (míng piàn); name (míngzi).

Initiation		Possible Response
English	**Chinese**	
What's your name? (to peer)	Qǐng wèn [nín] guì xìng?	Wǒ xìng Smith, jiào John, nǐ ne? Zhè shì wǒde míng piàn.
Pleased to meet you.	Xìnghuì. [Xìnghuì.]	Copy.
So glad to see you.	Hěn gāoxìng kàn dào nǐ.	Copy.
What's your name? (to kids)	Nǐ jiào shénme míngzi?	Wǒ jiào Smith John.
What are these [called]?	Zhège jiào shénme?	These are chicken feet. (Zhè shì jī jiǎo.)

• Salutations: Mr. = Xiānsheng; Ms. = Xiáojie; Mrs. = Nǚshì = Tàitai (informal).
• Chinese equivalent = Lǎo (old) Wáng, Xiǎo (little/young) Chén

A.5   Speak Chinese

Vocabulary: can (huì); speak (shuō); Chinese (zhōngwén); a little bit (yīdiǎnr); slow (màn).

English	Chinese	Possible Response
Can you speak Chinese?	Nǐ huì shuō Zhōngwén ma?	A little bit. (Huì yīdiǎnr.)
		I don't speak Chinese well. (Wǒde Zhōngwén shuō de bù hǎo.)
Please speak a bit slower.	Qǐng shuō màn yīdiǎnr.	Follow the request.

A.6 When people compliment you, then you should say …

English	Chinese
Thank you.	Nálǐ nálǐ. = Hǎo shuō, hǎo shuō. = Méiyǒula, méiyǒula. (It was nothing.) = Guò jiǎng, guò jiǎng. (You overly praised me.) = Bù gǎn [dāng], bù gǎn [dāng]. (I don't deserve.) = Bié (don't) kāi (crack open) wánxiào (joke) [le]. (Don't joke.)

Note that repeating is to increase the sincerity.

English	Chinese
Please don't say so! (a polite reply when praised)	Kuài (Hurry) bié (don't) zhème (so) shuō (say)!

A.7 Wishes and Exclamations

Vocabulary: wish (zhù); road (lù); smooth sailing (shùnfēng); happy (kuàilè); New Year (Xīn Nián); birthday (shēngrì); congratulations (gōngxǐ); may (yuàn); God (Shén); bless (zhùfú); my king (wú wang); long live (wàn suì); kidding/joking (kāiwánxiào).

English	Chinese
[Wish you] Have a good weekend!	Zhù nǐ yǒu yíge hǎo zhōumò!
[Wish you] Good luck.	Zhù nǐ hǎo yùn.
Have a good trip!	Yí lù (all the way) shùn (with) fēng (wind)!
Congratulations!	Gōngxǐ! = Gōngxǐ, gōngxǐ!
Merry Christmas!	Shèngdàn kuàilè!
Happy New Year!	Xīn Nián kuàilè!
Happy New Year! Congratulations and get rich!	Xīn Nián kuàilè! Gōngxǐ fā cái!
Happy birthday!	Shēngrì kuàilè!
May God bless you!	Yuàn Shén zhùfú nǐ!
TGIF (Thank God it's Friday)!	Gǎnxiè Shén jīntiān shì xīngqī wǔ!
Go! Go! Go!	Jiāyóu! Jiāyóu!
Wow! Fantastic/Excellent/Superb!	Wà! Hǎo bàng a!
Wow! You're really amazing!	Wà! Nǐ zhēn liǎobuqǐ!
Superb! / Outstanding!	Zhēn bàng!
Ouch! = Oh no!	Āiyōu! = Āiya!
What a surprise!	Āiyōu! = Yōu!
Bummer!	Zāogāo! = Zāo le! = Cǎn le!
Bummer! I forgot my wallet!	Zāogāo! (Zāo le!) Wǒ wàngjì le wǒde qiánbāo!
I'm dead! (I'm finished!)	[Wǒ] wán le!
Correct!	Duì! = Duì le! = Duì a! = Shì a!
Annoying!	[Zhēn] Tǎoyàn!
Really?!	Zhēn de [ma]?!
Never mind.	Suàn le. / Méi shì.

It stinks!	Chòu (stink) sǐ (to death) le!
It tastes aweful!	Nán (no good) chī (eat) sǐ (to death)/jí le!
You're kidding/joking?!	Nǐ kāiwánxiào?!
You're not kidding/joking?!	Nǐ méiyǒu kāiwánxiào ba?!
I'm so happy!	Wǒ gāoxìng (happy) jí (extremely)/sǐ (to death) le!
It's so funny!	Xiào (laugh) sǐ (to death) rén (people) le!
It got me so angry/mad!	Qì (angry) sǐ (to death) wǒ le!
Suit yourself!	Suí nǐde biàn!
Wait a minute/second/moment!	Děng yì děng!

A.8   In a restaurant

Vocabulary: eat (chī); finish (guò); full (chī bǎo); almost (chā bù duō).

Initiation		Possible Response
English	**Chinese**	**Possible Response**
What do you want to drink?	Nín xiǎng hē [diǎnr] shénme?	Píjiǔ hǎo le. (Beer is good.)
What do you want to eat?	Nín xiǎng chī [diǎnr] shénme?	Nín diǎn ba. (You order please.)
What would you like to order?	Nín xiǎng diǎn shénme?	Hǎo de (Okay), wǒ yào …
What do you have?	Nǐ yǒu shénme?	Wǒmen yǒu …
What is this?	Zhè shì shénme?	Zhè shì yúcì (shark fin).
I don't eat meat.	Wǒ bù chī ròu.	Méi wèntí, zhè **shì** sù de. (meatless)
I don't eat spicy stuff.	Wǒ bù chī là de dōngxi.	Méi wèntí, zhè **shì** bú là de. (not spicy)
Delicious!	Hǎo chī jí le!	Shì a! (Yes, it is!)
Are you full?	[Nǐ] chī bǎo le ma?	Mm … chā bù duō le. (Pretty much.)
Check please.	Qǐng jié zhàng.	Hǎo de. Yígòng shì … (The total is …)

A.9   The magic of 'hǎo'

hǎo [de] = okay = xíng = chéng = kéyǐ.

hǎo ba = okay, but with slight reluctance.

hǎo yìdiǎnr = a little bit more 'good' = better.

hǎo + adj. = so/very adj.		
English	**Chinese**	
So/Very cold/hot!	Hǎo	lěng/rè.
So/Very expensive!		guì.

Hǎo jí le!			
English	**Chinese**		
	adj.	adv.	emphatic
Excellent! Outstanding! Very well!	**Hǎo**	**jí** (extreme)	**le!**

hǎo + verb = pleasant to 'verb'		
English	**Chinese**	
It is pleasant to	eat.	**Hǎo**	chī.

	see/watch		kàn.
	listen.		tīng.
	play.		wán.
	use.		yòng.

hǎo + verb + jí le! = extremely pleasant to 'verb'!

English		Chinese		
		hǎo	verb	jí le!
It is extremely pleasant to	eat! (=Delicious!)		chī	
	see/watch!		kàn	
	listen!	Hǎo	tīng	jí le!
	play!		wán	
	use!		yòng	

Hǎo bù hǎo can be used in any situation where you are to ask for an opinion.

hǎo bù hǎo + verb?

English		Chinese	
		hǎo bù hǎo	verb?
Is it pleasant to	eat?		chī?
	see/watch/look?	Hǎo bù hǎo	kàn?
	listen?		tīng?
	play?		wán?

Note: **Hǎo bù hǎo** can also be used for asking for favor or permission when placed at the end of a sentence.

.... hǎo bù hǎo?

English		Chinese			
Let's go to	eat?	Wǒmen qù	chī (eat)	fàn (meal)	hǎo bù hǎo?
	a movie?		kàn (see/watch)	diànyǐng (movie)	
	a concert?		tīng (listen)	yīnyüè (music)	
	play ball?		dǎ (paly)	qiú (ball)	
Please lend me twenty dollars?		Qǐng jiè wǒ èrshí kuài **hǎo bù hǎo?**			
May we rest a moment?		Wǒmen xiūxí yíxià **hǎo bù hǎo?**			

verb + hǎo le = finished the verb

English	Chinese
We finished eating.	Wǒmen chī (eat) **hǎo le.**
I finished writing.	Wǒ xiě (write) **hǎo le.**

... hǎo le. = ... is good.

English	Chinese	Possible Response
What do you want to drink?	Nín xiǎng hē [diǎnr] shénme?	Píjiǔ **hǎo le.** (Beer **is good**.)
Which one do you want?	Nǐ yào nǎ yíge?	Zhège **hǎo le.** (This **is good**.)

		Zhè yíge **hǎo le**. (This one **is good**.)

A.10 In the class, the teacher may say …

Vocabulary: rest (xiūxi); minute (fēnzhōng); now (xiànzài); let's ([rang] wǒmen); #5 (dì wǔ); come together (lái); page (yè); study (xuéxí); read out loud (niàn); follow (gēn).

English	Chinese	Possible Response
Let's take 5.	Wǒmen xiūxi wǔ fēnzhōng.	Hǎo.
Give me five!	Gěi wǒ wǔ ge!	(follow the instruction)
Ready?	Hǎo le méi yǒu?	1) Hǎo le. (Ready.) 2) Jiù hǎo le. (Almost there.) 3) Hái méi yǒu. (Not quite.) 4) Méi yǒu. (Not at all.)
Do you understand?	[Nǐ] dǒng ma?	[Wǒ] dǒng. (I understand.) [Wǒ] bù dǒng. (I don't understand.)
Please close the door.	Qǐng guān mén.	Hǎo. / Shìde (Yes), lǎoshī (teacher).
Okay, now let's do …	Hǎo, xiànzài wǒmen zuò …	(follow the instruction)
Today, we study pinyin.	Jīntiān wǒmen xuéxí pīnyīn.	
Please turn to page 5.	Qǐng fān dào *dì wǔ* yè.	
Start from page x.	Cóng dì x yè kāishǐ.	
Please read.	Qǐng niàn.	
Please read after me.	Qǐng gēn wǒ niàn.	
Next one.	Xià yíge.	
Next time.	Xià yícì.	
Any questions?	Yǒu wèntí ma?	
Correct. Right. Yes.	Shì de. = Duì.	Bú shì de (incorrect) = Bú duì.
…, etc.	…, děng děng.	—

A.11 Where is the restroom?

English	Chinese
Where are you going?	Nǐ shàng nǎr qù?
I want to use the restroom.	Wǒ xiǎng (want) shàng/qù (go to) wèishēngjiān.
Where is the restroom?	Nálǐ shì wèishēngjiān (restroom)?

A.12 Making a phone call and leaving message

English	Chinese
Hello, I'm John Smith.	Wéi, wǒ shì Shǐmìsī Yuēhàn.
May I speak to Mr. Wang?	Wǒ néng hé Wáng xiānsheng jiǎnghuà ma?
Is Mr. Wang in?	Wáng xiānsheng zài ma?
It is he. / Speaking.	Wǒ [jiù] shì. (jiù: emphatic.)
He is in. Please hold.	Tā zài. Qǐng děngyíxià (wait a moment).
This call is for you, Mr. Wang.	Wáng xiānsheng nín de diànhuà.
Sorry, he is not in.	Duì bù qǐ. Tā bú zài.

Would you like to leave a message?	Nín yào liú yán/huà ma?
It's okay. I'll call back later.	Méi guānxi. Wǒ děngyíxià zài dǎ lái.
Okay. Please tell him …	Hǎo de. Qǐng gàosù tā ...
Thank you. Good bye.	Xièxie nín. Zàijiàn.
You're welcome. Good bye.	Bú kè qì. Zàijiàn.
Please call (v.) me.	Qǐng dǎdiànhuà gěi (to) wǒ.
Please give me a call (n.).	Qǐng gěi (to) wǒ yíge diànhuà.
Thank you for calling me.	Xièxie nǐ dǎdiànhuà lái.
Machine: Please leave a message. Bye!	Liú yán/huà jī: Qǐng liú yán/huà. Zàijiàn!
(1) This is Wáng Huá.	Zhè shì Wáng Huá.
(2) Sorry, I missed your call.	Duìbùqǐ wǒ méi jiēdào nínde diànhuà.
(3) Please leave your message. Thanks.	Qǐng liú yán/huà. Xièxie.
You dialed the wrong number.	Nǐ buō (dial) cuò (wrong) hàomǎ (number) le.

A.13   Instant Messenger (IM) and Email

Vocabulary: don't care (bù guǎn); idea (zhǔyì); later (huítóu); immediately (mǎshàng); again (zài); chat/talk (liáo); got to = must (děi); go (zǒu); back (huílái).

English	Chinese
Anyway! = Let it be!	Bù guǎn le!
Leave it alone. = Forget about it.	Bú yào guǎn tā.
Sure. = Certainly. = No problem.	Méi wèntí.
Of course. = Certainly.	[Nà] dāngrán le. / Hǎo de.
Good idea.	Hǎo zhǔyì.
I don't know.	Wǒ bù zhīdào.
I don't have the slightest idea/clue.	Wǒ méiyǒu yìdiǎnr zhǔyì.
Let's go fishing, what do you think?	Wǒmen qù diàoyú, nǐ kàn zěnmeyàng?
Not much (not a lot).	Méi shénme.
Why [is that]?	[Nà shì] wèishénme ne?
See you later.	Huítóu zài jiàn.
Talk to you later. (ttyl)	Huítóu zài liáo.
Got to go. (gtg)	Wǒ děi zǒu le.
I'll be right back. (brb)	Wǒ mǎshàng **jiù** huílái. (**bold**: emphatic) = Wǒ qù qù **jiù** lái.
I'll be right there.	Wǒ mǎshàng **jiù** qù.

A.14   Buy and Sell

Vocabulary: how much (duōshǎo); money (qián); stuff (dōngxī); cheaper (piányì [yì]diǎnr); pay (fù); cash (xiànjīn); give away free of charge (sòng); discount (dǎzhé); 10% discount (yī zhé); 80% discount (bā zhé).

English	Chinese				
I want to go to the <u>market</u> to buy stuff.	Wǒ yào qù	shìchǎng	mǎi		dōngxi.
I want to go to the <u>food market</u> to buy <u>food</u>.		cài shìchǎng			cài.
I want to go to the <u>supermarket</u> to buy <u>food</u>.		chāojí shìchǎng			cài.
I want to go to the <u>department store</u> to buy a necktie.		bǎihuògōngsī			lǐngdài.
I want to go shopping.	Wǒ yào qù mǎidōngxi / guàngjiē / gòuwù.				
How much is this? = How do you sell your stuff?	Zhège yào duōshǎo (how much) qián (money)?				
	Nǐde dōngxi (your stuff) zěnme mài?				
Too expensive!	Tài guì le!				
Can it be cheaper?	Néng piányì [yì]diǎnr ma?				
Please pay cash?	Qǐng fù xiànjīn.				
I don't want to buy it.	Wǒ bù yào mǎi le.				
Buy one get one free.	Mǎi yī sòng yī.				
I'll give you a **discount**.	Wǒ yào gěi nǐ **dǎzhé**. zhé = 10%				
How much of a **discount**?	**Dǎ jǐ zhé**? (jǐ = the number of **zhé**)				
20% off. (= You pay 80%.)	**Dǎ** bā (8) **zhé**. (8 x 10% = 80%)				

Appendix B

Vocabulary Building Blocks

This chapter covers the basic vocabulary building blocks that are frequently used in our daily conversations. Those include,

1. People: in a family, nationality
2. Numbers, counting method
3. Time, day, calendar, time order
4. Seasons, weather
5. Money, weight, length
6. Orientation, traffic directions
7. Transportation
8. Colors, sports
9. About the word 'good' (hǎo)
10. Unit words

To make best use of this chapter is to memorize it!

B.1.1   People in a Family (jiā rén)

man	woman	father	mother	son	daughter
nánrén	nǚrén	bàba	māma	érzi (nánér)	nǚ'ér
older brother	**younger brother**	**older sister**	**younger sister**	**bro. and sis.**	**child(ren)**
gēge	dìdi	jiějie	mèimei	xiōngdi jiěmèi	háizi(men)

uncle (younger than father)	**uncle** (older than father)	**aunt** (mother side)	**aunt** (father side)
shūshu	bóbo	āyí	gūgu

 Please check the dictionary for other relatives, such as grandparents, etc.

Example:

1) I have two children. This is my oldest (**lǎo dà**) and this is the second (**lǎo èr**).

2) My parents have three children, and I'm the youngest (**lǎo yāo**).

	dà	**èr**	**sān**	**...**	**yāo**
lǎo	oldest child	second child	third child	...	youngest child

Example:

1) My oldest brother (**dà gē**) is a teacher.

2) His third daughter (**sān nǚ'ér**) is an architect.

	gē (older brother)	**dì** (younger brother)	**jiě** (older sister)	**mèi** (younger sister)	**érzi** (son)	**nǚ'ér** (daughter)
dà	oldest					
èr	2nd					
sān	3rd					
...	...					
xiǎo	youngest					

B.1.2   Nationality (guójí)

Example: American = **Měi** + **guó rén** = **Měiguórén**.

Example: Canadian = **Jiānádà** + **rén** = **Jiānádàrén**.

	guó rén	country	**rén**	country	**rén**
Měi	American	**Jiānádà**	Canadian	**Pútáoyá**	Portuguese
Zhōng	Chinese	**Yìndù**	Indian	**Sūgélán**	Scottish
Yīng	English / British	**Yǐsèliè**	Israeli	**Xīnjiāpō**	Singaporean
Fǎ	French	**Yìdàlì**	Italian	**Xībānyá**	Spanish
Dé	German	**Rìběn**	Japanese	**Ruìshì**	Switzerland
Hán	Korean	**Bājīsītǎn**	Pakistani	**Tú'ěrqí**	Turkish
É	Russian	**Bōlán**	Poland	**Yuènán**	Vietnamese

B.2   Numbers (shùmù)

Example: 37 = **30** (top row) + **7** (left most column) = **sānshí qī**.

	10 (shí)	**20 (èrshí)**	**30 (sānshí)**	**...**	**90 (jiǔshí)**	**100 (yì bǎi)**
1 (yī)	11 (shí yī)	21 (èrshí yī)	31 (sānshí yī)		91 (jiǔshí yī)	101 (yì bǎi **líng** yī)
2 (èr)	12 (shí 'èr)	22 (èrshí 'èr)	32 (sānshí 'èr)			102 (yì bǎi **ling** èr)
3 (sān)	13 (shí sān)	23 (èrshí sān)				103 (yì bǎi **ling** sān)
4 (sì)	14 (shí sì)					
5 (wǔ)						
6 (liù)						
7 (qī)			37 (sānshí qī)			
8 (bā)						
9 (jiǔ)	19 (shí jiǔ)				99 (jiǔshí jiǔ)	
0 (líng)						110 (yì bǎi **yī shí**)

100 (yì bǎi)	110 (yì bǎi yīshí)	120 (yì bǎi 'èrshí)	...	1,000 (yì qiān)
101 (yì bǎi **líng** yī)	111 (yì bǎi yīshí yī)	121 (yì bǎi èrshí yī)		1,001 (yì qiān **líng** yī)
102 (yì bǎi **ling** èr)	112 (yì bǎi yīshí'èr)	122 (yì bǎi èrshí'èr)		1,002 (yì qiān **líng** èr)
...	...	...	...	...

English			Chinese		
10		**ten**	10		**shí**
100	one	**hundred**	100	yì	**bǎi**
1,000	one		1000	yì	**qiān**
10,000	ten	**thousand**	1,0000	yí	
100,000	one hundred		10,0000	shí	**wàn**
1,000,000	one		100,0000	yì bǎi	
10,000,000	ten	**million**	1000,0000	yì qiān	
100,000,000	one hundred		1,0000,0000	yí	
1,000,000,000	one		10,0000,0000	shí	**yì**
10,000,000,000	ten	**billion**	100,0000,0000	yì bǎi	
100,000,000,000	one hundred		1000,0000,0000	yì qiān	
1,000,000,000,000	one	**trillion**	1,0000,0000,0000	yí	**zhào**

0.25	líng **diǎn** (point) èr wǔ
3.1416	sān **diǎn** yī sì yī liù
2/3	Sān (3) **fēn** (part) **zhī** èr (2)
75/100 = 75%	bǎi (100) **fēn** (part) **zhī** qīshíwǔ (75)
20% off (English)	no Chinese counterpart
pay 80% (Chinese)	n.: bā (8) **zhé** (10%); v.: **dǎ** bā **zhé**
Ordinal (1st, 2nd, 3rd, ...)	1st = **dì** yī (1), 2nd = **dì** èr (2), 3rd = **dì** sān (3), ..., 100th = **dì** yìbǎi (100), etc.
Number 3 (#3)	**dì** sān **hào** = 3rd **number**
Page 7	**dì** qī **yè** = the 7th **page**
Phone number:	bā bā yī/yāo liù líng/dòng qī/guǎi èr. To avoid 'sound' error, we use 'yāo' for

881 6072	'1', 'dòng' for '0', and 'guǎi' for '7'.

Note: Other number related cases such as time, temperature, currency, weight, and length will be illustrated in the following sections.

B.3.1   Time (shíjiān)

Hour, Minute, & Second		
hour	**diǎn** (o'clock) = diǎnzhōng = shí (formal)	3:36:20 = sān (3) **diǎn**, sānshíliù (36) *fēn*, èrshí (20) *miǎo*
	xiǎoshí	Èrshí (20) xiǎoshí (hours). Used for telling a period of time.
minute	**fēn**	3:36:20 = sān (3) diǎn, sānshíliù (36) **fēn**, èrshí (20) *miǎo*
	fēnzhōng	Èrshí (20) fēnzhōng (minutes). Used for telling a period of time.
second	**miǎo**	3:36:20 = sān (3) diǎn, sānshíliù (36) *fēn*, èrshí (20) **miǎo**
	miǎozhōng	Èrshí (20) miǎozhōng (seconds). Used for telling a period of time.
quarter	**kè** (=15 minutes)	3:45 = sān diǎn sān (3) **kè**
half	**bàn** (=30 minutes)	5:30 = wǔ diǎn bàn; 30 minutes = bàn xiǎoshí (half an hour)
AM	**shàng wǔ**	Jīngtiān (Today) **shàng wǔ** (AM) shíyī (11) diǎn (o'clock) **zhěng** (sharp)
sharp	**zhěng**	wǒmen (we) yǒu (have) shēngrì (birthday) qìngzhùhuì (party).
PM	**xià wǔ**	Jīngtiān (Today) **xià wǔ** (PM) wǒmen (we) qù (go) dǎ qiú (play ball).
differ	**chā**	4:50 = **Chā** shí (10) *fēn* wǔ diǎn
pass	**guò**	5:10 = Wǔ diǎn **guò** shí *fēn*
much passed	**duō**	It is <u>much passed</u> *eleven* (*shíyī diǎn* **duō**), let's <u>go home</u> (*huí jiā*).

B.3.2   Time in A Day (zài yì tiān lǐ de shíjiān)

English		Chinese	Greetings
Early	morning	zǎochén, qīngchén	zǎoshàng hǎo, zǎo ān, zǎo
Mid		zǎoshàng	
Late		shàngwǔ	shàngwǔ hǎo
Noon		zhōngwǔ	wǔ ān
Afternoon		xiàwǔ	wǔ ān, xiàwǔ hǎo
Dusk		huánghūn	wǎn ān, wǎnshàng hǎo
Evening/Night		wǎnshàng	

B.3.3   Calendar (rìlì)

Example: **Sunday** = xīngqī rì/tiān or lǐbài rì/tiān

In a Week (xīngqī)						
Sunday	**Monday**	**Tuesday**	**Wednesday**	**Thursday**	**Friday**	**Saturday**

xīngqī	rì/tiān	xīngqī	yī	xīngqī	èr	xīngqī	sān	xīngqī	sì	xīngqī	wǔ	xīngqī	liù
lǐbài		lǐbài	(1)	lǐbài	(2)	lǐbài	(3)	lǐbài	(4)	lǐbài	(5)	lǐbài	(6)

Example: Wednesday, the 2nd = **èr hào**, xīngqī sān

In a Month (yüè)						
Sunday	**Monday**	**Tuesday**	**Wednesday**	**Thursday**	**Friday**	**Saturday**
		1 (yí **hào**)	2 (èr **hào**)	3 (sān **hào**)	4	5
6	7	8	9	10	11	12
13	14	15	16	17	18	19
20	21	22	23	24	25	26
27	28	29	30			

Example: Friday, **September** 25th = **jiǔ yüè** èrshíwǔ hào, xīngqī wǔ

In a Year (Nián)					
January	**February**	**March**	**April**	**May**	**June**
yí (1) yüè	èr (2) yüè	sān (3) yüè	sì (4) yüè	wǔ (5) yüè	liù (6) yüè
July	**August**	**September**	**October**	**November**	**December**
qī (7) yüè	bā (8) yüè	jiǔ (9) yüè	shí (10) yüè	shíyī (11) yüè	shí'èr (12) yüè

B.3.4   Time Order (shíjiān xiānhòu)

Example: yesterday = **zuó** (left most column) + **tiān** (top row) = **zuótiān**.

	tiān (day)	**nián** (year)	x = yüè (month), xīngqī (week), zhōumò (weekend), xīngqī # (weekday)
dà dà qián	the day before **dà qián tiān**	—	—
dà qián	the day before **qián tiān**	—	—
qián	the day before **yesterday**	the year before last year	—
zuó	**yesterday**	—	—
qù	—	last year	—
jīn	today	this year	—
míng	**tomorrow**	next year	—
hòu	the day after **tomorrow**	the year after next year	—
dà hòu	the day after **hòu tiān**	—	—
dà dà hòu	the day after **dà hòu tiān**	—	—
shàng shàng ge	—	—	the x before last x
shàng ge	—	—	last x
zhè ge	—	—	this x
xià ge	—	—	next x
xià xià ge	—	—	the x after next x

Note that theoretically 'dà', 'shàng', and 'xià' can be applied to as many times as you want so long as the communication is effective.

B.4.1 Seasons (jìjié)

Example: Spring = chūnjì (Spring season) or chūntiān (Spring day).

Spring		Summer		Fall (Autumn)		Winter	
Chūn	jì (season)	xià	jì (season)	qiū	jì (season)	dōng	jì (season)
	tiān (day)		tiān (day)		tiān (day)		tiān (day)

Chūnjié (Spring Festival), Duānwǔjié (Dragon Boat Festival), Zhōngqiūjié (Moon Festival)

B.4.2 Weather (tiānqì / qìhòu)

Sunny sky (qíngtiān)	Jīntiān (today) shì [yíge (a) dà (big, no cloud at all)] qíngtiān.
Cloudy sky (yīntiān)	Jīntiān (today) shì yíge yīntiān.
Rain (noun: yǔ)	dà yǔ (big/heavy rain), xiǎo yǔ (small/light rain), máomao yǔ (drizzle).
Rain (verb: xià yǔ)	Tiān (Sky=It) zài (progressive tense) xià yǔ. (It is raining.)
Rainy day (xiàyǔ tiān)	Jīntiān (today) shì yíge xiàyǔ tiān (rainy day) = Today is a rainy day.
Sleet (bīngpáo)	Tiān (Sky=It) zài (progressive tense) xià bīngpáo. (It is sleeting.)
Snow (xuě)	Zuótiān (yesterday) xià le (downed) yì chǎng (unit) dà (heavy) xuě.
Storm (bàofēngyǔ)	Lóngjuǎnfēng (tornado), jùfēng (hurricane), táifēng (typhoon)
Humid (cáoshī)	Shànghǎi de qìhòu (weather) hěn cáoshī.
Temperature (wēndù)	Jīntiān de wēndù shì duōshǎo (how much)?
Degree (dù)	Shèshì (Celsius) 23 dù (degree) / Huáshì (Fahrenheit) 73 dù.
Hot (rè)	Shànghǎi de tiānqì zěnmeyàng (how)? Yòu (not only) rè yòu (but also) cáoshī.
Cold (lěng)	Zhège fángjiān (room) yǒu [yī]diǎnr lěng. (This room is a little cold.)

B.5.1 Money (qián)

RénMíngBì = RMB (¥)	1 yuán = 10 jiǎo = 100 fēn; bàn = half yuán
	In spoken language, 'kuài' replaces 'yuán,' and 'máo' replaces 'jiǎo.'
	Yuán, jiǎo, fēn are Units for money, for example, ¥ 5 = wǔ kuài (unit) qián (money)
¥ 13.6	Shísān kuài liù [máo]
¥ 21.64	Èrshíyī kuài liù máo sì [fēn]
¥ 52.5	Wǔshí'èr kuài wǔ [máo]; Wǔshí'èr kuài bàn (half kuài)

B.5.2 Weight (zhòngliàng)

1 jīn (斤) = 500 grams (gōng kè, 公克)	1 jīn (斤) = 16 liǎng (兩)

Example: Zhè kuài (unit) niúròu (beef) yǒu (has) yì jīn (斤) wú liǎng (兩) zhòng (weight).

B.5.3 Length (chángdù)

1 km (gōng lǐ, 公里) = 0.621 mile (yīng lǐ, 英里) = 2 lǐ (里, Chinese mile)
1 m (gōng chǐ, 公尺) = 3.281 foot (yīng chǐ, 英尺) = 3 chǐ (尺, Chinese foot)

Example: Yì lǐ (里) děngyú (equals) 1,500 chǐ (尺) děngyú 1,641 yīng chǐ (英尺, foot).

B.6   Orientation (fāngwèi)

Example: center = **zhōng** (left most column) + **xīn** (top row) = **zhōngxīn**. 'Top' can be **shàngmiàn** or **shàngtou** or **shàngbiān**.

	miàn	tou	biān	jiān	xīn
shàng	top	top	top	—	—
xià	bottom, next	bottom	bottom	—	—
zuǒ	left	—	left	—	—
yòu	right	—	right	—	—
lǐ	Inside	inside	inside	—	—
wài	outside	outside	outside	—	—
qián	front	front	front	—	—
hòu	back	back	back	—	—
[zhèng] duì	opposite	—	—	—	—
xié duì	diag. opposite	—	—	—	—
páng	—	—	side	—	—
zhōng	—	—	—	middle	center

Example: come (specifyee) up (specifier) = **shàng** (left most column) + **lái** (top row) = **shàng lái**

	qù (away from speaker)	lái (toward speaker)	x = Transportation: **chē** (vehicle), **fēijī** (airplane), etc.	x = class (**kè**), work (**bān**), etc.	yuè (month), xīngqī (week)
shàng	go up	come up	get on x	go to x	previous
xià	go down	come down	get off x	finish x	next
qǐ	—	get up	—	—	—
jìn	go in	come in	—	—	—
cū	go out	come out	—	—	—
guò	go there	come over	—	—	—
huí	go back	come back	—	—	—

Example: turn on x = **kāi** (left most column) + **[kāi]** (top row) + x (object) = **kāi [kāi] x**.
Shàng, kāi, and diào are Result Adverbs, and they are optional in this group of applications.

	[shàng]	[kāi]	[diào]	x (object)	English
kāi	—	turn on	—	x = device = radio, faucet, light, etc.	turn on x
guān	—	—	turn off		turn off x
kāi	—	open	—	**mén** (door, cover, etc.)	open the x
guān	close	—	—	**mén** (door, cover, etc.)	close the x

Example: open x = **dǎ** (left most column) + **kāi** (top row) + x (object) = **dǎ kāi x**.

	—	kāi	—	x (object)	English
dǎ	—	open	—	x = door, cover, box, etc.	open x

Example: above = **yǐ** (left most column) + **shàng** (top row) = **yǐshàng**.

	shàng	**xià**
yǐ	above	below

upstairs	**downstairs**	**go upstairs**	**go downstairs**
lóushàng	lóuxià	shàng lóu	xià lóu

	miàn	**biān**	**fāng**
dōng	east side		eastern
xī	west side		western
nán	south side		southern
běi	north side		northern

before …	**after …**	**next to …**
zài … yǐqián	zài … yǐhòu	zài … gébì

B.7 Traffic Directions (jiāotōng fāngxiàng)

Example: turn left = **zuǒ** (left column) + **zhuǎn** (top row) = **zuǒ zhuǎn**

	zhuǎn (turn)		**lùkǒu**
zuǒ (left)	turn left	**shízì**	intersection
yòu (right)	turn right	**dīngzì**	'T'

go straight	**go through**	**go around**	**pass by**	**toward**
yìzhí zǒu	chuān guò	rào guò	jīng guò	wǎng

traffic light	**southeast side**	**northwest side**
hónglǜ dēng	dōngnán biān	xīběi biān

B.8 Transportation & Traveling (yùnshū hé lǚxíng)

Example: car = **qì** (left column) + **chē** (top row) = **qìchē** (very often 'qì' is dropped)

	chē
qì	car
kǎ	truck
pǎo	sports car
huǒ	train
zìxíng	bicycle
mótuō	motorbike
sānlún	tricycle
gōnggòng qì	bus
tǎnkè	tank
xiāofáng	fire truck

jiùhù	ambulance
chūzū	taxi
rénlì	rickshaw
mǎ	wagon

airplane	all vessels	boat	big ship	ocean liner	warships
fēijī	chuán	tǐng	lúnchuán	yóulún	jūnjiàn

reservation	yùdìng		airport	fēijīchǎng
ticket agent	piàowùyüán		train station	huǒchē zhàn
ticket	piào		bus station	gōngòngqìchē zhàn
one-way	dānchéng		passport	hùzhào
round-trip	láihuí		visa	qiānzhèng
seat	zuòwèi		customs	hǎiguān
itinerary	xíngchéng		depart	qǐchéng
lavatory/restroom	wèishēngjiān/cèsuǒ		arrive	dàodá

B.9.1 Colors (yánsè)

	black	red	yellow	green	blue	brown	violet	gray	white
n.	hēisè	hóngsè	huángsè	lǜsè	lánsè	zōngsè	zǐsè	huīsè	báisè
adj.	hēi de	hóng de	huáng de	lǜ de	lán de	zōng de	zǐ de	huī de	bái de

B.9.2 Sports (yùndòng)

Example: baseball = **bàng** (left column) + **qiú** (top row) = **bàngqiú**

	qiú
bàng	baseball
lán	basketball
zú	soccer
měishì zú	football (U.S.)
wǎng	tennis
pīnpāng	table tennis
yǔmáo	badminton

pái	volleyball
bīng	hockey
gāo'ěrfū	golf

ballpark	swim	auto race	Olympic Games	ski	skate
qiúchǎng	yóuyǒng	sàichē	Ào yùnhuì	huáxüě	huábīng

B.10 Good (hǎo)

English	Chinese
so so	hái hǎo / mǎmǎhūhū
good	hǎo

better	gèng hǎo
very good	hěn hǎo
best	zuì hǎo
excellent	fēicháng hǎo hǎo jí le tài hǎo le
overly + adj.	adj. de bù de liǎo
overly good (=excellent)	hǎo de bù de liǎo
better and better	yüè lái yüè hǎo (good)
faster and faster	yüè lái yüè kuài (fast)
the faster the better = as soon as possible	yüè kuài yüè hǎo

You may put 'bu' before the Chinese phrase to negate.

B.11   Unit Words (liàng cí)

A unit word is used for counting a noun. The format is: Number + Unit Word + Noun. For example in 'I have <u>five cats</u>,' the <u>five cats</u> = wǔ (five) + zhī (unit word) + māo (cat).

Unit Words	The nature for the Noun	Examples
bǎ	something with handles	yì **bǎ** jiǎndāo (scissor), yì **bǎ** yǔsǎn (umbrella)
bān	scheduled transportation	xià yì **bān** fēijī. (next flight)
bāo	*a package of*	yì **bāo** yīfú (clothing)
bēi	*a cup of*	yì **bēi** chá (tea)
běn	in book shape	yì **běn** shū (book)
bǐ	(business) deal	yì **bǐ** shēngyì (business deal)
bù	movie	yí **bù** diànyǐng (movie)
cān	meal	sān **cān** fàn (meal) = three meals
céng	floor	wǔ (5) **céng** lóu (story)
chǎng	for games, shows	yì **chǎng** qiúsài (ball game)
dǎ	*a dozen of*	yì **dǎ** jīdàn (chicken egg)
dài	*a bag of*	liǎng (2) **dài** píngguǒ (apple)
dào	dish, test question	yí **dào** cài (dish); wǔ **dào** shì tí (test question)
dī	*a drop of*	yì **dī** (a drop of) xüě (blood)
dǐng	only for hats	yì **dǐng** màozi (hat)
duǒ	only for flowers	yì **duǒ** huā (flower)
fèn	in paper bundle shape	wǔ **fèn** bàogào (report)
fēng	only for letters	yì **fēng** xìn (letter)
ge	a broad usage unit word	wǔ **ge** rén (people); liǎng (2) **ge** píngguǒ (apple)
hé	*a box of*	liǎng **hé** tángguǒ (candy)
jiā	an establishment	yì **jiā** gōngsī (company)
jià	for big machine	yí **jià** fēijī (airplane)
jiàn	garment	sān (3) **jiàn** yīfú (clothing); yí **jiàn** kùzi (pants)

jié	class	Jīntiān wǒ yǒu sān **jié** kè. (Today I have 3 classes.)
kē	for plants, trees	yì **kē** shù (tree)
kǒu	family member	Wǒ jiā yǒu wǔ **kǒu** rén. (My family has 5 members.)
kuài	in pieces	liù (6) **kuài** táng (candy)
liàng	for vehicles only	wǔ **liàng** qìchē (car)
liè	for train only	yí **liè** hǒuchē (train)
mén	for courses	sān **mén** kè (courses/classes)
miàn	flags, mirror	yí **miàn** qízi (flag); wǔ **miàn** jìngzi (mirror)
pán	*a plate of*	yì **pán** suǐguǒ (fruits)
pī	horse	yì **pī** mǎ (horse)
piàn	in slice shape	sān **piàn** miànbāo (bread)
píng	*a bottle of*	yì **píng** píjiǔ (beer)
qǘn	*a herd of*	yì **qǘn** niú (cow); liǎng **qǘn** yáng (sheep)
sāo	only for ships	wǔ **sāo** chuan (ship)
shàn	door, window	yí **shàn** mén (door); yí **shàn** chuānghu (window)
shuāng	in pairs	sān **shuāng** wàzi (socks); liǎng **shuāng** xiézi (shoes)
suǒ	the unit for schools	yì **suǒ** xüéxiào (school)
tái/bù	related to machine	yì **tái/bù** diànnǎo (computer)
táng	class	Jīntiān wǒ yǒu sān **táng** kè. (Today I have 3 classes.)
tiáo	in rope shape	yì **tiáo** shéngzi (rope); liǎng **tiáo** xiāngjiāo; yì **tiáo** hé (river)
tǒng	*a bucket of*	yì **tǒng** suǐ (water)
tóu	cow, pig	wǔ **tóu** niú (cattle)
wǎn	*a bowl of*	sān **wǎn** fàn (rice)
wèi	people	sān **wèi** loǎshī (teacher)
zhǎn	only for lamps	yì **zhǎn** dēng (lamp)
zhāng	in paper shape	wǔ **zhāng** zhǐ (paper)
zhī (支)	in stick shape	sì (4) **zhī** qiānbǐ (pencil)
zhī (只)	unit for insects, animals	wǔ (5) **zhī** yáng (sheep)
This table is not exhaustive.		

Appendix C

Amusing Skits for Fun & Practice

In this chapter, we have provided a few practical and funny skits for your amusement and practice. In previous chapters, we have examined the direct correlation, cross correlation, and culture-specific relationships between Chinese and English. As you will see, each skit line may include one, two, or all three characteristics. In addition, we have blended in Chinese history and cultural elements.

We encourage students to memorize and act out the skits to establish useful lines for real situations, and perhaps to entertain friends and colleagues. They may also be used as the end-of-course skit presentation to show how much progress students have achieved. For now, let's enjoy the skits!

C.1 A Big Invention (Dà Fāmíng)

Setting

On a nice summer evening, two next-door neighbors are mowing their lawns. While taking a break they start to chat about the odor released from the weeds …

A	The odor of the weeds stinks.	Zhácǎo de wèidào chòu sǐ le.
B	Yes! What a nuisance!	Shì a! Zhēn tǎoyàn!
A	They are everywhere.	Tāmen dàochù dōu shì.
A	I want to have them all killed!	Wǒ yào bǎ tāmen dōu shāsǐ!
A	Oh, by the way, are you not a *biologist*?	O, duì le, nǐ bú shì yíge *shēngwùxuéjiā* ma?
B	Yes. Why?	Shì de. Wèishénme?
A	I have a good idea.	Wǒ yǒu yíge hǎo zhǔyì.
B	What idea?	Shénme zhǔyì?
A	Can you do a research *making* a grass to release fruit or flower scent when you cut it?	Nǐ néng bù néng zuò yíge yánjiù *shǐ* cǎo fàngchū suǐguǒ huò huā de qìwèi dāng nǐ gē tā de shíhòu.
B	Good idea! It's difficult but possible.	Hǎo zhǔyì! Suīrán kùnnán dànshì yǒu kěnéng.
B	But it must be able to repell bugs as well.	Dànshì tā bìxū yě néng qū chóng.
A	Yes, of course.	Shì de, dāngrán le.
A	So then, when you cut your grass, we will smell rose fragrance.	Nàme, dāng nǐ gē nǐde cǎo de shíhòu, wǒmen huì wéndào méiguì de xiāngwèi.
B	When you cut your grass, we will smell watermelon.	Dāng nǐ gē nǐde cǎo de shíhòu, wǒmen huì wéndào xīguā.
A	Ha ha. When we smell jasmine,	Ha ha. Dāng wǒmen wéndào mòlìhuā de shíhòu,
A & B	that must be Mr. Jones!	nà yídìng shì Jones xiānsheng le!
A & B	Ha ha ha ha ha ha ha …	Ha ha ha ha ha ha ha …

C.2 A Story about Contradiction (Guānyǔ MáoDùn de Gùshì)

Setting

At an ancient day flea market …

Merchant	Spear! Shield! Spear! Shield! …	Máo! Dùn! Máo! Dùn! …
Merchant	The *best* spear and shield in the world!	[Zài] shìjiè shàng *zuì hǎo de* máo hé dùn.
Customer	How much is (=How do you sell) your spear?	Nǐde máo zěnme mài?
Merchant	1,000 per spear.	Yìqiān kuài yì zhī.
Customer	So expensive! Theirs were sold for *only* 200.	Zhème guì! Tāmende *zhǐ* mài liǎngbǎi kuài.
Merchant	But my spear is the sharpest.	Kěshì wǒde máo zuì lì.
Merchant	It can penetrate anything.	Tā néng chuāntòu rènhé dōngxi.
Customer	How much is (=How do you sell) your shield?	Nǐde dùn zěnme mài?
Merchant	2,000 per shield.	Liǎngqiān kuài yíge.

Customer	Too expensive! Theirs were <u>sold for</u> *only* 500.	Tài guì le! Tāmende *zhǐ* <u>mài</u> wúbǎi.
Merchant	But my shield is the *hard<u>est</u>*.	Kěshì wǒde dùn <u>zuì</u> *yìng*.
Merchant	It can block <u>anything</u>.	Tā kěyǐ dǎngzhù <u>rènhé</u> dōngxi.
Customer	So, <u>can you</u> use your spear to penetrate your shield?	Nàme, <u>nǐ néng bù néng</u> yòng nǐde máo chuāntòu nǐde dùn ne?
Merchant	Well …	Wǒ …

C.3 A Story of Yàn Zi (Yàn Zi de Gùshì)

Setting

During the Chūnqiū Age, about 700 BC, China consisted of many small warlord countries. A short but very smart man, Yàn zi, was Qí Guó's ambassador to Chǔ Guó. Looked down upon by Chǔ Guó's reception offcials, one day when Yàn zi arrived at Chǔ Guó, they decided to let Yàn zi enter through a small door. Now, Yàn zi is standing before a tiny door and looks puzzled. …

Yànzi	What? This is a door <u>for dogs</u>.	Shénme? Zhè shì yíge <u>gěi gǒu</u> de mén.
Yànzi	**Only** a dog country uses dog doors.	**Zhǐyǒu** gǒu guó **cái** yòng gǒu mén.
Yànzi	I [have] *come to* a people country, <u>right</u>?	Wǒ *lái dào* yíge rén guó, <u>duì ma</u>?

Embarrassed, the reception officials lead him through a formal gate. Later, he is at a meeting with the emperor. The emperor again mocks him for his shortness …

Emperor	I thought Qí Guó was a big country <u>with many people</u>.	Wǒ xiǎng Qí Guó shì yíge <u>yǒu xǔduō rén</u> de dà guó.
Yànzi	Yes, we are a big country, and <u>of course</u> we <u>have many people</u>.	Shì de, wǒmen shì yíge dà guó, <u>dāngrán</u> wǒmen <u>yǒu xǔduō de rén</u>.
Emperor	But why do they <u>send you here</u>?	Dànshì wèishénme tāmen <u>pài nǐ dào zhèlǐ lái **ne**</u>?
Yànzi	<u>Our country</u> has a very strict rule.	<u>Wǒ[men de] guó</u> yǒu yíge hěn yángé de guīzé.
Yànzi	Good people are sent to good countries, and bad people are sent to bad countries.	Hǎo rén bèi pài dào hǎo guó, Huài rén bèi pài dào huài guó.
Yànzi	Therefore, this is why I [have] come here.	Suǒyǐ, zhè **jiù** shì wèishénme wǒ lái zhèlǐ.
Emperor	#?%*$#! …	#?%*$#! …

C.4 A Story of Kǒng Róng (Kǒng Róng de Gùshì)

Setting

Kǒng Róng is Confucius' 24th generation offspring. He is a great man in Chinese history, and this is one of his many stories. Kǒng Róng was well known for his great wisdom. When he was ten years old, one day he went with his father to visit a prominent government official (Lǐ Yīng) while another scholar (Chén Wěi) was also visiting. As father and son enter the sitting room, the father greets Lǐ and Chén …

Father	Good morning, Mr. Lǐ.	Zǎo, Lǐ xiānsheng.
Father	Good morning, Mr. Chén.	Zǎo, Chén xiānsheng.
Lǐ	Good morning. Mr. Kǒng.	Zǎoshànghǎo, Kǒng xiānsheng.
Chén	Good morning. Mr. Kǒng.	Nín zǎo, Kǒng xiānsheng.
Lǐ	Long time no see. Mr. Kǒng. How are you?	Hǎo jiǔ bú jiàn. Kǒng xiānsheng. Nín hǎo ma?
Father	Not [too] bad, just busy, busy, busy.	Hái bú cuò, xiā máng (blind busy).
Father	(toward the son) Hurry, greet people!	Kuài jiào rén!
Son	Hello uncle Lǐ.	Lǐ buóbuo hǎo.
Son	Hello uncle Chén.	Chén shūshu hǎo.
Lǐ	I'm well, good boy.	Hǎo, hǎo, hǎo (= guāi = behave) háizi.
Chén	I'm well. You are a kid <u>with manners</u>.	Hǎo, nǐ shì yíge <u>yǒu lǐmào</u> de háizi.

Lǐ turns to the father and says, …

Lǐ	I <u>heard</u> your boy is **both** smart **and** obedient.	Wǒ <u>tīng shuō le</u> nǐde háizi **jì** cōngmíng **yòu** xiàoshun.
Father	Thank you. You're so kind.	Nálǐ, nálǐ. Nín guò (overly) jiǎng (praised) le.
Father	He [also] <u>misbehaves</u> *sometimes*.	Tā *yǒushíhòu* yě <u>bùguāi</u>.
Lǐ	I think he must be the material of <u>high officials</u> *in the future*,	Wǒ xiǎng tā *jiānglái* yídìng shì <u>gāo guān</u> de cáiliào,
Lǐ	<u>like</u> Mr. Chén.	<u>xiàng</u> Chén xiānsheng <u>yíyàng</u>.

Envy churns inside scholar Chén …

Chén	Well, if a person is very smart <u>at childhood</u>, this person *may not be good* <u>after growing up</u>.	Rúguǒ yíge rén <u>zài xiǎo de shíhòu</u> hěn cōngmíng, zhège rén <u>zhǎng dà yǐhòu</u> *kěnéng bù hǎo*.

Kǒng Róng slowly responded …

Son	Yes, sir. I think you must have been very smart <u>when</u> you were young.	Shìde, shūshu. Wǒ xiǎng <u>dāng</u> nǐ xiǎo de <u>shíhòu</u> yídìng hěn cōngmíng.
Chén	#%*$#! …	#%*$#! …

C.5 Real Confused and Fake Smart (Zhēn Hútú hé Jiǎ Cōngmíng)

Setting

Real Confused (Zhēn Hútú) and Fake Smart (Jiǎ Cōngmíng) are two friends. One day, Real Confused wants to buy a pair of shoes, and he asks Fake Smart about what to do …

Real	I want to buy <u>a pair of</u> shoes.	Wǒ xiǎng mǎi <u>yì shuāng</u> xiézi.
Real	<u>There are</u> so many shoes <u>in the shoe store.</u>	<u>Yǒu</u> zhème duō de xiézi <u>zài xié diàn lǐ.</u>
Real	<u>What</u> *should* I <u>do</u>?	Wǒ *yīnggāi* <u>zěnme zuò/bàn</u> ne?
Fake	Very simple.	Hěn jiǎndān.
Fake	You first *cut out your foot shape* <u>on paper</u>,	Nǐ xiān <u>zài</u> zhǐ <u>shàng</u> *jiǎn chū* nǐde jiǎo xíng,

	then take it *to* the shoe store.	ránhòu ná [tā] *qù* xié diàn.
Real	Which [one] foot?	Nǎ yì zhī (zhī: unit for foot) jiǎo?
Fake	Both.	Liǎng zhī [dōu (all) yào (need)].
Real	Great! Thanks.	Hǎojíle! Xièxie.

Real Confused takes his foot cut-outs showing up at the store, and he realizes that he has two left feet. Rushing his way back home to cut a right foot, he comes across Fake Smart ...

Fake	Didn't you buy the shoes?	Nǐ mǎi le xié méiyǒu?
Real	I didn't.	Méi yǒu.
Fake	Why?	Wèishénme [ne]?
Real	I have cut two left feet.	Wǒ jiǎn le liǎng zhī zuǒ jiǎo.
Fake	You are really confused.	Nǐ zhēn hútú.
Fake	But I have a good idea.	Kěshì wǒ yǒu yíge hǎo zhǔyì.
Real	What is it?	Shì shénme ne?
Fake	If you cut two right feet, you can buy two pairs!	Rúguǒ nǐ jiǎn liǎng zhī yòu jiǎo, nǐ jiù néng mǎi liǎng shuāng le!
Real	Wow! That's a good idea!	Wa! Zhēn shì yíge hǎo zhǔyì!
Real	No wonder you're so smart.	Nán guài nǐ zhēn cōngmíng.
Fake	Thanks!	Nálǐ! Nálǐ!

C.6 Haggling (Tǎojià Huánjià)

Setting

On a cool and comfortable afternoon, Mr. and Mrs. Smith are browsing in a flea market, relaxed but with a mind for serendipity. Suddenly, a flash of light catches Mrs. Smith's eyes while a peddler stands behind a busy display of gold watches. Mrs. Smith immediately falls in love with a watch and asks Mr. Smith to show his haggling prowess in buying it. Mr. Smith acquiesced ...

Mr. S	How much is this watch?	Zhè zhī biǎo [shì] duōshǎo qián?
Peddler	800 RMB.	Bābǎi kuài.
Mr. S	Too expensive!	Tài guì le!
Peddler	Not at all, sir.	Yìdiǎnr dōu bú guì, xiānsheng.
Peddler	Theirs are sold for 1,000 RMB!	Tāmende mài yìqiān kuài ne!
Mr. S	Can it be cheaper?	Néng piányì yīdiǎnr ma?
Peddler	No problem.	Méi wèntí.
Peddler	You're guests from a *foreign country*.	Nǐmen shì cóng *wài guó* lái de kèrén.
Peddler	I'll give you *50% off*. How's 400 sound?	Wǒ [yào] gěi nǐ *wǔ zhé*, sì bǎi zhěnmeyàng?
Mr. S	It is still too expensive!	Hái shì tài guì le!
Peddler	So then, you just give me a *number*.	Nàme, nǐ **jiù** gěi wǒ yíge *shùmù* ba. (jiù: emphatic)
Mr. S	100, otherwise I don't want to buy it.	Yìbǎi, fǒuzé wǒ **jiù** bú yào mǎi le. (jiù: emphatic)
Peddler	What! Sir, mine is a small business,	Shénme! Xiānsheng, wǒde shì yíge xiǎo shēngyì,
Peddler	I'll lose money, sir.	Wǒ yào péi qián le, xiānsheng.

As Mr. and Mrs. Smith are about to turn around and leave, …

| Peddler | Is this graceful lady your daughter? | Zhè wèi yōuyǎ de xiǎojie shì nǐde nǚér ma? |

Mrs. Smith is flattered, happy, and smiling. …

Mr. S	No, she is my wife.	Bú shì de, tā shì wǒde tàitai.
Peddler	Sorry! She looks not only young but also beautiful.	Duìbùqǐ! Duìbùqǐ! Tā kànqǐlái yòu niánqīng yòu piàoliang.
Peddler	She looks like a movie star.	Tā kànqǐlái xiàng yíge diànyǐng míngxīng.
Mrs. S	Oh! Hush your mouth!	O! Méiyǒula! Méiyǒula!
Peddler	You're welcome, Ma'am.	Búkèqì, tàitai.
Peddler	Sir, how does 200 sound?	Xiānsheng, liǎngbǎi zhěnmeyàng?
Peddler	I can't reduce it anymore.	Bù néng zài jiǎn le.
Mr. S	100!	Yìbǎi!
Peddler	Sir, Mine is a small business.	Xiānsheng, wǒde shì yíge xiǎo shēngyì.
Peddler	I rely on this to feed my whole family.	Wǒ yīkào zhège yǎnghuó wǒde quán jiā.
Peddler	My business is very difficult to do.	Wǒde shēngyì hěn nán zuò.
Mrs. S	Sweetheart, pity the poor man a little.	Tiánxīn, tóngqíng zhège kělián de rén yìdiǎnr ba.
Mrs. S	Just give him 200, I'm hungry and tired.	Jiù gěi tā liǎngbǎi ba, wǒ yòu è yòu lèi.
Mr. S	Alright. Here is 200.	Hǎo ba. Zhè shì liǎngbǎi kuài.
Peddler	Thank you sir! Thank you Ma'am!	Xièxie [nǐ] xiānsheng! Xièxie [nǐ] tàitai!

Picking up the gold watch in a glassy box, Mrs. Smith is elated and leans toward Mr. Smith and says, …

Mrs. S	Sweetheart, you really are a haggling expert.	Tiánxīn, nǐ zhēn shì yíge tǎojià huánjià de zhuānjiā.
Mrs. S	You are my hero.	Nǐ shì wǒde yīngxióng.
Mr. S	No big deal, honey.	Méi wèntí, mìtáng.
Mr. S	For you, I will do anything.	Wèi le nǐ, wǒ yùanyì zuò rènhéshì.

As the good evening continues. …

C.7 Whatever (Suíbiàn)!

Setting

John and Ann have just finished a Saturday matinee. Standing in the theater lobby, …

Ann	How was the movie, honey?	Diànyǐng hǎo bù hǎo kàn?
John	Not bad. Luckily, there were subtitles.	[Hái] bú cuò. Hǎozài yǒu zìmù.
John	Otherwise, I could not understand it at all.	Fǒuzé, wǒ jiù wánquán kàn bù dǒng le.
Ann	They spoke too fast.	Tāmen shuō de tài kuài le.
Ann	The leading man is handsome, but a little girly.	Nán zhǔjiǎo hěn yīngjùen, dànshì yǒu yìdiǎnr niángniángqiāng.

John	The *leading woman*'s kung fu is really <u>not bad</u>.	*Nǚ zhǔjiǎo* de gōngfū zhēn <u>bú cuò</u>.
John	I'm hungry. Let's get something to eat?	Wǒ è le. Wǒmen suíbiàn chī diǎnr ba?
Ann	I'm hungry. Let's get something to eat?	Wǒ è le. Wǒmen suíbiàn chī diǎnr ba?
John	<u>Okay</u>, what do you want to eat?	<u>Hǎo de</u>, nǐ xiǎng chī diǎnr shénme?
Ann	Anything.	Suíbiàn.
John	Excellent! I know a <u>small eatery</u>.	Hǎojíle! Wǒ zhīdào yíge <u>xiǎo chīdiàn/fànguǎn</u>.
John	They <u>have</u> the best <u>noodles</u> *in town*.	Tāmen yǒu *chénglǐ* zuìhǎo de <u>miàn shí</u>.

John and Ann arrive at the eatery. Upon entering, …

Hostess	Hello. How many?	Nín hǎo. Jǐ wèi?
John	Two. Non-smoking please.	Liǎng wèi. Bù xīyān.
Hostess	<u>Certainly</u>, please *follow* me.	<u>Hǎo de</u>, qǐng *gēn* wǒ <u>lái</u>.
John	Thank you.	Xièxie [nǐ].

At the table, the waiter takes orders for drinks …

Waiter	What do you want to drink, ma'am?	Nín xiǎng hē [diǎnr] shénme, <u>xiǎojie</u>?
Ann	Hmm, <u>a glass of</u> red wine, please.	Hmm, qǐng **lái** <u>yì bēi</u> hóng jiǔ.
Waiter	<u>Of course</u>, and you, sir?	<u>Hǎo de</u>, nín ne, xiānsheng?
John	**Give** me <u>a bottle of</u> Chinese beer, please.	Qǐng **gěi** wǒ **lái** <u>yì píng</u> Zhōngguó píjiǔ hǎo le.
Waiter	<u>Coming right up</u>!	<u>Mǎ shàng</u> **jiù** <u>lái</u>!

At the table, the waiter takes orders for the meal …

John	Sweetheart, what would you like to eat?	Tiánxīn, nǐ xiǎng chī shénme?
Ann	Whatever.	Suíbiàn.
Ann	I want to <u>use the restroom</u>.	Wǒ xiǎng <u>shàng wèishēngjiān</u>.
John	No problem.	Méi wèntí.

Ann goes to the restroom and John turns to the waiter …

John	<u>Okay</u>, I'll *order* <u>for the lady</u>.	<u>Hǎo de</u>, wǒ yào <u>tì xiǎojie</u> *diǎncài*.
John	Please give her a 'seafood noodle.'	Qǐng gěi tā yíge 'hǎixiān miàn.'
John	**Give** me a 'beef noodle' and two 'scallion pan cakes.'	**Gěi** wǒ **lái** yíge 'niúròu miàn' hé liǎngge 'cōng yóubǐng.'

As the two are drinking and chatting, the waiter comes with the food …

Waiter	Here are your 'beef noodle' and 'scallion pan cakes,' sir.	Zhè shì nǐde 'niúròu miàn' hé 'cōng yóubǐng,' xiānsheng.
John	Thanks.	Xièxie.
Waiter	Here is your 'seafood noodle,' ma'am.	Zhè shì nínde 'hǎixiān miàn,' xiǎojie.

The waiter leaves as Ann looks on at her food and frowns …

| Ann | What? Seafood? | Shénme? Hǎixiān? |
| Ann | You know I don't like squid. | Nǐ zhīdào wǒ bù xǐhuān yóuyú. |

John	But didn't you say 'whatever'?	Dànshì nǐ **bú shì** shuō 'suíbiàn' **ma**? (chap. 5)
Ann	Yes, but you <u>should have known</u> *by now* that I don't like squid.	Shì de, dànshì nǐ *xiànzài* <u>yīnggāi yǐjīng zhīdào</u> <u>wǒ</u> bù xǐhuān yóuyú.
John	Sorry, I forgot. Please <u>don't</u> be upset.	Duìbùqǐ, wǒ wàng le. Qǐng <u>bú yào</u> shēngqì.
John	How about this, you eat mine, and I eat yours? Okay?	Zhè yàng ba, nǐ chī wǒde, wǒ chī nǐde? Hǎo ma?
Ann	Hmm, okay.	Hmm, hǎo ba.

In fact, 'Niúròu Mian' and 'Cōngyóubǐng' have unexpectedly saved the night.

C.8   Self Introduction

Sample lines (not arranged sequentially)

Exchange names

1	How are you?	Nín hǎo ma?
2	May I ask, what is your name?	Qǐng wèn nín guì xìng?
3	My name's _____.	Wǒ jiào <u>last name, first name</u>.
4	And you?	Nín ne?
5	My surname is _____ and called _____.	Wǒ xìng <u>surname</u> jiào <u>first name</u>.
6	This is my business (**name**) card.	Zhè shì wǒde **míng** piàn.
7	Thank you.	Xièxie nín.
8	You're Mr. Wang. **Pleased to meet you!**	Nín shì Wáng xiānsheng. **Xìnghuì! Xìnghuì!**

Telling where I'm from

1	I'm an American.	Wǒ shì [yíge] Měiguórén.
2	I'm <u>from</u> New York.	Wǒ <u>cóng</u> Niǔ Yuē <u>lai</u>.
3	New York is a big city and maybe <u>as big as</u> Shanghai.	Niǔ Yuē shì yíge dà chéngshì, yěxǔ <u>gēn</u> Shànghǎi <u>yíyàng dà</u>.
4	Where are you from?	Nín cóng nálǐ lái?
5	Have you been to New York?	Nín qù guò Niǔ Yuē ma?
6	Welcome to America.	Huānyíng dào Měiguó lái.
7	I live at …, and my address is…..	Wǒ zhù zài …, wǒde dìzhǐ shì …
8	My phone number is …, email address is …	Wǒde diànhuà shì …, diànzǐyiújiàn shì …

My profession

1	I'm a software engineer.	Wǒ shì yíge ruǎnjiàn gōngchéngshī.
2	I'm a programmer.	Wǒ shì yíge chéngxùyuán.
3	I'm a reporter.	Wǒ shì yíge jìzhě.
4	My expertise is <u>in …</u> design.	Wǒde zhuānmén shì <u>zài …</u> de shèjì.
5	Are you a manager?	Nín shì jīnglǐ ma?

My family

1	I have five siblings.	Wǒ yǒu wǔ ge xiōngdìjiěmèi.
2	I have two older brothers, one younger brother, one older sister, and one younger sister.	Wǒ yǒu liǎngge gēge, yíge dìdi, yíge jiějie, hé yíge mèimei.
3	Are you married?	Nǐ jiéhūn le ma?
4	Do you have children?	Nǐ yǒu háizi ma?
5	I have one son and one daughter.	Wǒ yǒu yíge érzi hé yíge nǔ'er.
6	How old are they?	Tāmen duó dà le?
7	One is 10 and one is 12.	Yíge shí, yíge shí'èr.

My hobby

1	Do you have a hobby?	Nǐ yǒu shìhào ma? / Nǐde shìhào shì shénme?
2	My hobby is …	Wǒ de shìhào shì ….
3	Playing music is my hobby.	Wánr yīnyüè shì wǒde shìhào.
4	I like to read.	Wǒ xǐhuān kànshū.
5	I like to fish.	Wǒ xǐhuān diàoyǘ.
6	I like to play golf.	Wǒ xǐhuān dǎ gāo'ěrfū qiú.
7	I like to eat pizza, play TV games, watch movies, and sleep.	Wǒ xǐhuān chī pizza, dǎ diànshì (TV) yiúxì, kǎn diànyǐng, hé suìjiào.

My education

1	I graduated from … in 2000.	Wǒ zài 2000 nián cóng … bìyiè.
2	I have two majors. One is Computer Science, another is Electrical Engineering.	Wǒ yǒu liǎngge zhuānyiè, yíge shì diànnǎo, yíge shì diànjī.

My favorite food

1	My favorite food is *Chinese food (cuisine)*.	Wǒ zuì xǐhuān de shíwù shì *Zhōngguó cài*.
2	Mongolian BBQ is good (*not bad*).	Ménggǔ kǎoròu hěn hǎo (*bú cuò*).
3	I like spicy beancurd and *hot and sour soup*.	Wǒ xǐhuān mápó dòufu hé *suān là tāng*.
4	I am a vegetarian.	Wǒ shì yíge sùshízhě (= Wǒ chī sù).
5	I like beer.	Wǒ xǐhuān píjiǔ.
6	Heaven Palace's food is excellent!	Heaven Palace de cài hǎo chī jí le!

My favorite sport

1	My *favorite* sport is *football*.	Wǒ *zuì xǐhuān* de yùndòng shì Měishì zúqiú.
2	Do you play tennis?	Nǐ dǎ wǎngqiú ma?

My Chinese ability

1	I don't speak Chinese well.	Wǒde Zhōngwén shuō de bù hǎo.

2	I can speak <u>a little bit of</u> Chinese.	Wǒ huì shuō <u>yīdiǎnr</u> Zhōngwén.
3	I can listen, speak, read and write some Chinese.	Wǒ huì tīng, shuō, dú hé xiě yīdiǎnr Zhōngwén.
4	I can listen and speak some Chinese.	Wǒ huì tīng hé shuō yīdiǎnr Zhōngwén.
5	I can't read and write Chinese.	Wǒ bú huì dú yě (also) bú huì xiě Zhōngwén.
6	I understand Chinese TV.	Wǒ kàn de dǒng Zhōngwén diànshì.
7	I understand some Chinese TV.	Wǒ kàn de dǒng yīdiǎnr Zhōngwén diànshì.
7	I don't understand Chinese TV <u>at all</u>.	Wǒ <u>wánqüán</u> kàn bù dǒng Zhōngwén diànshì.

Index for Chapter 8 Culture-Specific Words & Phrases

English to Pīnyīn

The ones without English counterparts are listed below (not exhaustive):

Pīnyīn to English

Vocabulary Index

English to Pīnyīn

Pīnyīn to English

Printed in the United States
138044LV00001B/109/P

9 780615 210445